With best wishes,

In the Truth!

[signature]

31 July 2007.

Ken Cooke

After leaving Percy Jackson's Ken, a miner's son, became a biologist and a graduate member of the Institute of Export. During a career in the international chemical industry – largely with the French multinational Rhône-Poulenc – he travelled widely and for some years specialised in sugar cane agronomy. He developed a special affinity for the Caribbean and Latin America.

Since retiring Ken has organised a series of bilateral reunions, celebrating the school's exchanges with Germany in the 1950s. As well as German, he converses in three other European languages.

In October 2004, he and his old German exchange partner Heinz Wartenberg featured on BBC Radio 4's "Home Truths", discussing with John Peel their fifty years of Anglo-German friendship.

HISTORY OF THE PERCY JACKSON GRAMMAR SCHOOL

Adwick-le-Street, Doncaster, Yorkshire

1939-1968

Recollections of Schooldays
Of the 1940s, 1950s & 1960s

Edited by
Ken Cooke

Matador
9 De Montfort Mews
Leicester LE1 7FW, UK
Tel: (+44) 116 255 9311 / 9312
Email: books@troubador.co.uk
Web: www.troubador.co.uk/matador

ISBN 978-1905886-784

Typeset in 12pt Bembo by Troubador Publishing Ltd, Leicester, UK
Printed in the UK by The Cromwell Press Ltd, Trowbridge, Wilts, UK

Matador is an imprint of Troubador Publishing Ltd

For our Grandchildren

Patrons

David Cranshaw, Kathleen Gibson Pumfrey, Mary Hart Hutchinson
Mollie Peet Jenkins, Roy Jackson
Audrey Harrison Roberts, Raymond Hide, Ernie Roberts

John Hudson, Geoff Gravil, Angela Harrison Beckett

Margaret North Cook, David 'Kruk' Pulman, Tony Parkin
Audrey Westgarth Collishe (now Lomer), Keith Swinscoe
Barbara Knight Brooks, Barrie Clark, Albert Locker, Edgar Fuller
John Flory

Margaret Pidcock Burns, Brian McGarrigle, Marion Walker Rodwell
Maureen Brown Crosby, Norman Wainwright, Christine Ashby Bell
Margaret Skinner Griffiths, Vicki Jackson West

Terry McGarrigle, Catherine Dick & David Skelton
Janet Kitson & John Roberts

Dave Etchell, Gary Goodlad, Joan Crane Moffet
Lynn Oakland & Gary Hepworth

Paul Edwards

*Some patrons have contributed in the memory of particular
teachers and pupils of the School.*

Contents

CHAPTER 3
MEMORABLE EVENTS & ACHIEVEMENTS   49

In chronological order: 1939-1968

CHAPTER 4
CULTURAL BACKGROUND TO THE 40s, 50s & 60s   65

Errors and Omissions

At the outset I thought it might be feasible to to sketch thumbnails of all or most of the school's teachers, but when I had identified and counted them I realized this would be impracticable – there had been about 210. My calculations also showed that around 3,500 pupils passed through the school. The *History* clearly could not aim to report on so many individuals, so this work is what its title suggests – a *history of the school* – the story of the body, the life and the ethos of the Percy Jackson Grammar School.

I recognise that the school continued after August 1968 as the new comprehensive, Adwick School, and indeed many of the teachers stayed on, but I chose to restrict this work to the time when it was a state grammar school.

My contributors and I have tried our best to be faithful to the facts. By the nature of the project there will inevitably be some errors and omissions and insofar as these affect any reader's role in the *History* I apologise most sincerely.

Similarly, no-one – pupil or teacher – should take too seriously any perceived adverse personal comments in the text. After all, they are merely the views of half-educated children recalled after forty and fifty years and more!

KC

Acknowledgements

This was always going to be a work of collaboration and I am most happy to acknowledge the offerings of so many willing helpers, representing both pupils and teachers. Throughout the text contributors are identified by name or more often by initials which are listed in a key at the end. Some people remembered more than others but I thank them all. Likewise I acknowledge the help, advice and support of many people whose names do not appear as contributors.

I felt especially privileged to make contact with several of the "founding" pupils from the early years. Kathleen (Gibson) Pumfrey, Roy Jackson and David Cranshaw were particularly helpful, as also was Norman Staveley, representing the war-time evacuees of Riley High School, Hull. For someone of my vintage, contact with the later generations too has been very refreshing.

I must signal the outstanding contributions of two colleagues:

Margaret North Cook for the many hours spent in Doncaster Archives and elsewhere trying to make sense of the records - and of my endless queries - and for her constant support throughout the preparation.

Brian "Mac" McGarrigle, our transatlantic correspondent, for his many and detailed personal recollections and especially for his "socio-philosophical contribution" (my caption) which constitutes Chapter Four: *Cultural Background*.

I also thank Ron Cockroft, PE & Games teacher, for his constructive comments on parts of the draft and for still managing to motivate me after all these years.

I thank Doncaster Archives and the Doncaster Chronicle for giving access to their records.

It seems usual nowadays to acknowledge the indulgence of one's spouse and children. Mine were just happy I was out of the way! I do not believe I was more burdensome to them than usual.

Last, but not least, I thank my Patrons for supporting this private publication.

Ken Cooke
Ilkley, Yorkshire
December 2006

Foreword

A Former Pupil

Former PJGS pupils and teachers owe Ken a debt of gratitude for putting together this splendid piece of social history. In response to an invitation to provide a short foreword to his fascinating and informative book *HISTORY OF THE PERCY JACKSON GRAMMAR SCHOOL*, I can do no better than repeat what I wrote to Ken after first reading the draft I received in early 2006:

"I was particularly struck by the moving way you succeed in capturing the pluses as well as the minuses of life in those days, without losing a light touch. Like many ex-PJGS pupils who have strayed far from their roots, for some years I have felt a strong desire to convey, somehow, to my children and grandchildren some idea of what life was like when I was growing up. All of us are in your debt for doing the main part of the job for us, in a way that would be hard to equal, let alone better.".

Raymond "Spike" Hide - Washington House, PJGS, 1940-47
Professor Emeritus of Physics, Oxford University
East Molesey, Surrey; December 2006.

A Former Teacher

I feel honoured and privileged to have been asked by the author to write a foreword to his book.

It was in September 1949 that with some trepidation I joined the staff of the

Percy Jackson Grammar School. I had been offered a post at my old grammar school on the edge of the Lake District the same week as my interview at Percy Jackson's. As I was then living in West Yorkshire I chose to come to Woodlands. For some time I wondered if I had made the right decision, but I think I did - as I spent the rest of my career there.

I stayed for two reasons – the pupils and the staff. Percy Jackson's was not an ancient educational establishment. It was only ten years old when I joined and its total life spanned only thirty years, but the generally friendly and positive attitude of the pupils and the dedication of the staff throughout its life, both in the classroom and in the many extra-curricular activities, helped to provide for its pupils a solid educational base on which to build a rewarding and satisfying adult life.

I commend Ken for the tremendous amount of time and effort he has put into producing this book. Many of the anecdotes recorded will no doubt bring back happy memories to both staff and pupils. May the book be treasured by those fortunate enough to read it.

Ron Cockroft MC – Teacher of Physical Education & Games,
PJGS 1949-1968
South Elmsall, Yorkshire; December 2006.

Preface

Conception

"Schooldays are the best days of your life. Discuss".
Schooldays were certainly good – well, in parts – and probably more fun in retrospect than they were at the time.

I saw this undertaking as an opportunity to combine the chronology of an institution with a goodly helping of nostalgia and sentiment - not just the dry dates and events, but something much less formal, reflecting personal experiences and achievements - small and great: "Once more with feeling."

Gestation

With a small group of old Percy colleagues I helped in 1999 to organise a bilateral reunion of former pupils who had participated in the Anglo-German school exchanges of 1953 and 1954. Incidentally, it was my perceived gubernatorial role in subsequent reunions which earned me the reputation and sobriquet of "Grand Vizier".

This first reunion resulted in a successful and happy event in Doncaster in August 2000 when 35 German friends came across the North Sea to lodge at the Earl of Doncaster Hotel. The first item on our programme was a visit to the old school, which I for one had not visited for over forty years. And - you know, it was just the same - at least the central block, that is. The main entrance, the assembly hall, the two parallel wings of classrooms, the quadrangles and the dining hall were just as I remembered them, perhaps showing their age – but so was I!

Being at school again, it was inevitable that we discussed memories of the old days: "You remember when...? and Who was it that...? and That Miss Whatsit, she was so... Whatever happened to So-and-So?" I came to realize that many of us had such favourable memories of our time at the school and of the quality of the education we received there. To this day, one of our number (RB) finds the opportunity at any gathering to declare that *"At Percy's we had the best education imaginable"*. More than this, of course, were the friendships and camaraderie we experienced during those formative years, much of which were to be lost, or suspended, as we embarked on our separate careers.

I did know that the former state grammar school had become a comprehensive school but I did not know when exactly it had happened. During this visit to the school I learned that the conversion date was August 1968. My next thought was that this meant the old grammar school existed for just twenty-nine years – three decades – and that I and my peers were slap in the middle (1950-58). It thus occurred to me that writing a history covering only twenty-nine years ought to be very doable.

Then in early 2004 I happened to meet Barbara Fox, a founding first former of 1939, and now living in our town, Ilkley in West Yorkshire. I mentioned the idea of writing a history and she recalled some of her memories of the school in wartime and of the evacuee "Hull boys", which I found fascinating. This decided me and I put together a framework of dates and notes and invited others to produce the *History*, hoping that people with a more literary background than mine – in history, the arts or the media – would volunteer. Alas to no avail! So it falls to a biologist to present *Percy Jackson's - History of The Percy Jackson Grammar School*.

Birth
Evolution, reproduction and fossils are what biologists do. Enjoy!

Work on this History began in April 2004: KC

Introduction

The Percy Jackson Grammar School
This lino-cut featured in many editions of the School Magazine.

Adwick-le-Street

The School is named after Alderman Sir Percy Jackson, a very active proponent of education on the West Riding of Yorkshire County Council in the 1920s and 1930s. It is located in a coal-mining area in the village of Adwick-le-Street, about 8 km north of Doncaster and adjacent to the Great North Road (part of the A1 until the Doncaster by-pass opened in 1961) which is derived from the original Roman road, Ermine Street. "Le-Street" in a place name usually denotes being sited on a Roman road. Indeed, there are still remnants of a track called the Roman Ridge to the west of the old A1 running from the Sun Inn at Sunnyfields, behind Highfields and Woodlands to Red House.

The school was situated between two roads with connections going back to feudal times: Windmill Balk Lane and Tenter Balk Lane. A balk was an unploughed area in the medieval three-field system, designed to provide access to the cultivated areas. (We learned all this from "Chas" in the first form: KC). The school's location was more popularly known as Woodlands, which was the name of the modern village built to accommodate the miners working at nearby Brodsworth Main colliery. Brodsworth Main was known as "The Queen's Pit" since it supplied coal to Buckingham Palace. Less than a mile to the other side of the school was another mine, Bullcroft, whose spoil heaps – "the Black Alps" – were visible from the school's grounds.

The church of St Lawrence in the village of Adwick-le-Steet dates from the 12th Century. In the 16th and 17th Centuries Adwick Hall was occupied by the Washington family. It was from a branch of this family which George Washington, first president of the United States, was probably descended (EB).

This *History* covers the period from the school's opening in October 1939 until it closed as a state grammar school in July 1968, when it became a comprehensive school.

Sir Percy Jackson J P, LLD 1869–1941

Percy Richard Jackson was educated in Huddersfield. In 1890 he joined the firm of Field & Botterill solicitors in Skelmanthorpe, retiring in 1927. He was a member of the West Riding County Council for some thirty years, where his particular interest was education. For many years he was chairman of the West Riding Local Education Authority and from 1918 he was a member of the Court of Leeds University. He was made a knight in 1925 and received an honorary LL.D degree from Sheffield University in 1926.

Sir Percy was a member of the government appointed consultative committees for the Hadow Reports on education in 1926 and 1933. He opened nearby Maltby Grammar School in April 1932 and also the Dinnington Senior Boys and Senior Girls Schools in 1935.

He died in 1941 at his home "Woodlands", at Scisset near Skelmanthorpe, Yorkshire.

The Scholarship or 11 Plus Exam

In the last year of primary – also called junior – school, when they were ten or eleven years old, the more able children were entered around February for the "Scholarship" exam, known after 1944 as the "11 Plus". For many years this comprised three papers: English, Maths and "Intelligence" – problem solving. In the thirties and early forties passing this exam not only secured a place at a grammar school but also paid towards the fees – the County Minor Scholarship (DOM). This was formalised between the pupil and the County Council in a "Special Place Award Agreement" and if the pupil dropped out of school the parents were liable to refund a year's tuition fees of nine guineas (£9.45) (KRG). With the advent of state grammar schools, fees were no longer involved and passing the exam simply entitled one to a place at grammar school.

But what price progress? Some twenty years later, the editorial of the Balkite 1960-61 considered "The abolition of fee paying has had the strange result of making people value grammar schools less because no one is any longer compelled to pay for the privilege. The development of the welfare state, looking after the citizen from the cradle – and before – to the grave seems to benumb initiative, hard work and ambition." (The editor must have been reading the *Daily Mail* that week! KC.)

Typically around a half of final year juniors were entered for the exam and perhaps under half of them would pass. In this way around twenty percent of children were "creamed off" to grammar school. The large majority of children therefore continued their education in Secondary Modern schools. Waiting for the results to be announced could be a stressful time. Obviously, if you had hopes of getting to grammar school but failed the exam you and your parents could be very disappointed. However, there were one or two ways round this. One was to stay on another year at primary school or even proceed to the secondary modern school for a year and take the exam again. Another option after one or more years in the secondary modern was take the exam for the Technical College which placed more emphasis on vocational subjects and offered another route to qualifications and further education.

The Scholarship or 11 Plus scheme was clearly divisive – it was designed to be! Throughout the 1950s argument rose against the unfairness of determining a child's educational future at such an early age - as well as denying the majority of children access to a good education. After its election in 1964, the Labour Government encouraged local authorities to introduce comprehensive schools to which all children were admitted without a selection exam. That is to say, without regard to ability. Many authorities opposed this new system at first – indeed some still do. Likewise when the Conservatives were elected in 1970, they chose to leave decisions on reorganisation to local authorities (EB). The Percy Jackson Grammar School became a comprehensive school, Adwick School, in August 1968.

The Economic Climate (KC)

As pupils who passed the "Scholarship" or "11 Plus Exam", we were the recipients of a grammar school education "free at the point of delivery", which our parents regarded as a great benefit. They would have been unlikely to afford the fees associated with the previous system. After covering essential food and housekeeping costs most working-class families of that era had very little surplus from their weekly wage.

Some families were so stretched materially or economically that they needed their older children to help out at home, especially if mother became ill. In the context of the time, this tended to affect girl pupils more than boys. In his report at the prize-giving of 11th November 1949, Headmaster Mr Elliott, referring to absences from school was reported as saying: "Perhaps the greatest handicap to steady progress was that many of our older pupils had been kept away from school to help in the home, and he earnestly asked parents who had the real welfare of their children at heart to cooperate in this problem." (SM 1949-50)

It might sound like a "sob story" but times were very hard for the working class. Times had always been hard for the working class and, whilst we hardly noticed it, in the post-war decades things definitely began to improve.

Nevertheless, in the 40s and 50s an outfit of clothes had to last a year – if not two. We tended to have two sets of clothes: "best" and "everyday": "everyday" being last year's "best", unless it had become ridiculously small – always a risk. Making, repairing and altering clothes was a normal part of mother's life – sewing a tear, taking in a frayed cuff, adjusting a hem, darning socks, turning a worn shirt collar, mending a burst seam, patching elbows of jackets and seats of trousers. Only in the late 50s did we start to consider and to buy additional, non-essential items of clothing more for enjoyment or "fashion" – or vanity? - what in later decades were to become known as "leisure wear". (See also Chapter 4: Clothes)

During and immediately after World War II we were encouraged at school to write small, not to leave spaces and always to use both sides of the page so as to economise in the use of paper. This clearly was as much to do with the national economy as with the family housekeeping. Of course, inflation and the rise in incomes make comparisons difficult, not to mention the change to decimal currency in 1971. "Old money" consisted of a pound containing 20 shillings, with each shilling having 12 pence. Thus the pound held 240 old pence (d) as against 100 new pence (p) after conversion. A new penny is therefore worth 2.4 old pence – or pennies.

In the early 1950s a pupil was unlikely, unless he was going away on holiday, to have more than a shilling in his pocket or purse. This equates to five new pence in 21st Century money. For a child, the bus fare into town was about two old pence (less than one new penny in today's money), a full-size Mars bar four pence (but they were bigger then) and an icecream cornet (now "cone") was three pence. Roy Jackson claims a better deal was to order two penn'orth of icecream in a mug, which with two wafers would provide an icecream sandwich $1^1/_2$ inches (3.7 cm) thick!

Dad's weekly wage was around £7 to £10 and the rent would typically be around 30/- (thirty shillings or £1.50) to £2 per week. Practically no mining family owned their own home and the vast majority lived in rented houses belonging either to the pit or to the council. When I was a

Saturday butcher's boy in 1952, a good joint of beef cost ten shillings (50 new pence) and I was paid five shillings (25 new pence) for a morning's work. A major menswear chain famously promoted suits at fifty shillings (£2.50 in decimal).

It seems Rock'n Roll changed all that! From around 1955 there appears to have been a marked increase in disposable income. Cause or effect?

CHAPTER 1

1939 A New State Grammar School

The school, in new purpose-built premises, "opened for instruction" on 9 October 1939 just a few weeks after the start of World War II. One supposes the timing was not planned that way. A Dedicatory Service was held on the 9 October with introductory remarks by the Chairman of the Governors, County Alderman J W Lane JP, followed by prayers and hymns conducted by the rector of Adwick-le-Street, the Rev S A Taylor (IMN). On the opening day building had not finished and much work continued, largely on the first floor (EO). The wooden panels in the main hall were still being applied and academic classes were held in the woodwork and metalwork rooms and in the teachers' common rooms (RJ). The school was not officially opened until 23 October 1943, some four years later (SR).

The programme for the Official Opening (from NSS) describes the premises as comprising 21 acres (8.5 hectares), of which the buildings, associated grounds and gardens occupied 3 acres (1.2 hectares). The two-storey building was designed to accommodate 540 pupils and was constructed of steel framing, bearing concrete floors and flat roofs. The total cost of the site, buildings and equipment was approximately £62,000.

The first pupils were very impressed with "this amazing new building...
with science labs, special subject rooms, lecture theatre, gymnasium etc. It
was light, airy and with attractive colour schemes" (MH). The lavish wash-
basins and cloakroom facilities were impressive, at least to the nine pupils
from Carcroft (RJ). The school was held to be a shining example for the
West Riding and there was even a rumour that a swimming pool had
been planned for the area which became occupied by the air raid shelters.
(MPJ)

It was a co-educational (boys and girls) state grammar school, selecting pupils
on ability based on what was to become the notorious "Scholarship" or "11
Plus Exam" (see Introduction), but at the time we pupils just took it for
granted. The main educational aim of the school's curriculum was to prepare
pupils, by the age of 15 or 16, for the School Certificate – "School Cert."
After that, the academically ambitious could continue for two years in the
sixth form to take the Higher School Certificate. It is worth recalling that
only in 1947 was the school leaving age raised from 14 to 15.

From 1951 "School Cert" was replaced by GCE – the General Certificate of
Education – which was graded at two levels: "Ordinary" or GCE O-level at
age 16 and "Advanced" or GCE A-level at age 18 at the end of the sixth
form. Results at "O" and "A" level represented qualifications for jobs or for
further education. Younger readers might question where GCSE – General
Certificate of Secondary Education – comes into the picture. Well, this was
introduced much, much later - in 1986.

The first Headmaster was Mr Ronald Field 1939-1945 and the first Senior
Mistress cum Assistant Head was Miss Hellena Todd 1939-1942. Chairman
of the Governors was Alderman J W Lane who served until 1958 (School
Magazine 1957/58).

The original intake consisted of only 85 pupils, being 62 into the 1st year
(two classes, 1H & 1B) , 11 into the 2nd year and 12 into the 3rd year (SR).
Pupils for the second and third years were transferred from other grammar
schools in the area (EO). It was the members of the 1939 third year intake
which constituted the first upper sixth year in 1943-44, at the end of which
four students gained their Higher School Certificate.

The curriculum for the first year included two 45-minute periods per week in which pupils could elect to study any of the wide range of subjects offered by the staff - the so-called Dalton Plan. The theory was that voluntary study would be diligent study, but results must have been disappointing, as the scheme perished. The nearest we came to it, in later years, were Private Study periods - during which "Grandad" Moore often ran his football pool or we played "Hangman", "Battleship" and other high-level educational pastimes. (RJ)

Creating the original cricket pitch was very much a community endeavour. Following the hiring of a permanent groundsman, Mr Constable (probably 1940), there was a great deal of shovelling, raking and rolling to be done...and most of us took part. It was a pretty good pitch - which is more than could be said for those at some other schools where we competed. (RJ)

For the first few years, progress was reported to parents on a monthly basis. Good performance was measured by a system of "Credits" and bad, by the awarding of "Debits". Lots of credits would produce a blue report; lots of debits generated a (shudder) pink one, and those lurking in the middle got a white one. It still seems a sound system to me today, although the paper-work load on teachers must have been burdensome. I don't think this practice survived more than a couple of years. Of course, the annual report was one that gave the teachers more licence to indulge their creativity as they summarised the year's performance. Good examples are to be found in Ian Hay's "The Housemaster". (RJ)

The **school badge** and motto and the school rules were devised by the first members of staff (MH). In the badge, the shield is divided vertically into two fields: left are the red and white vertical stripes of the Washington family of Adwick-le-Street and right are the three white roses of the West Riding on a green field. The motto is *"Keep Troth"*.

The school was unusual in teaching German as first foreign language, as it was considered to be an important language for science and technology. Originally the first year class titles contained the initial of their form teacher, eg 1H with Miss Homan and 1B with Mr Belton (MH). From the second year, French was also taught. Equal weight was given to arts and science "streams", the specialisms being reflected in class titles. After the War the three classes of each year, after the first year, were streamed **L**anguages, **S**cience and **P**ractical. By the late forties with four classes per year: AL, BL for the language stream and AS, BS for the science stream. Originally Latin was not taught, but from the mid-40s it was available from the fourth form to some of the language pupils, with the exam being taken in the lower sixth (DOM). In the late forties it was offered from the third form in preparation for GCE o-level in the fifth. From the early 1950s fewer pupils were streamed into the specialisms and a "general" stream was introduced, with class titles of GA and G (KC).

Pupils were drawn from the local communities and reflected the dominance of the coal-mining industry. In the days of "King Coal" it is probably true to say that the school was built to educate the children of miners and a large majority of pupils came from mining families. The rest came from other parts of the local economy - shopkeepers, artisans, farmers and railway workers. The expansion of coal mining in Yorkshire had attracted workers from many other parts of the country, especially from the older mining areas. In its early years many of the school's pupils were the children of incomers from areas as diverse as the North Midlands, Lancashire, Scotland, Wales and the North East.

At that time there was a distinct administrative separation between Doncaster Borough, being the town, and Doncaster Urban District with the Don Valley Rural District, representing the surrounding villages – which were mainly coal-mining communities. The Percy Jackson Grammar School served Don Valley Rural District along with the Bentley and Adwick wards of Doncaster Urban District (FJA) and consequently had quite a different source of pupils from the town's Doncaster Grammar School which served the borough with its much wider mix of industries, trades and professions. There is a certain irony in the "rural district" comprising largely industrial communities. On the other hand, coalmines were originally sunk on green-field sites with fields and woods all around them – just witness "Woodlands" as the name of the early 20th century colliery village! (KC)

But this has all been reported before by some anonymous wag in the School Magazine of 1947:

*"**Here beginneth the first chapter of the Epistle of St Percy, the son of Jack:***

At this time, in the country of the trees, near the city of the Donne, there exists a building overfilled with people of many clans.

Yea, they are gathered together even from the clan of Bentley, and the clan of Skellow, and the clan of Askern.

And here they are united in tribes, yea, verily the first tribe – this being the last – and the second tribe, even up to the sixth tribe. But the first tribe has overflowed into the land of their neighbours.

And there are appointed elders in authority over them, each of his own religion, yea, even of the B1 sect and the D1 sect, and the sect of many tongues.

And the elders war with each other for the souls of the tribes, yea, especially for the second and third tribes."

Writing in 1947, it is significant that he says that the building was "overfilled" and that the first form overflowed into a neighbouring school.

First caretaker: Mr Jeffries and his wife occupied the caretaker's house at the school gate on Windmill Balk Lane. Mr Jeffries was fatally electrocuted whilst working in the boilerhouse. Mrs Jeffries received an electric shock when she touched the body (BF). The next caretaker was Mr Craig, with Mrs Craig as kitchen manager.

World War II 1939–1945

A number of male teachers including Mr Belton (art and woodwork), Mr Milson (maths and senior master) and Mr Emmott (history and scripture) were drafted into the forces during the war years. (BF,RJ). Indeed, during the war all boys became eligible for conscription on reaching their 18th birthday. After the War they were obliged to serve two years of National Service. Under certain conditions military service could be deferred until after college or university. Thus, for example, our later physics teacher, Alan Dixon, took a concentrated degree course at Birmingham University before joining the army. From September 1942 to June 1944 he was required to study every weekday from 9 to 5 and Saturdays 9 to 12. All spare time and the summer break were taken up with Senior Training Corps (military) activities. Then he went into the army on war service. National Service ended in 1958 and boys born from 1940 onwards were not required to register.

In the middle of the War it became apparent that the nation needed more coal and from December 1943 until the end of the War ten percent of conscripts were sent to work in the mines as "Bevin Boys". Notable Bevin Boys from the north of England included comedian Eric Morecambe, actor Lord Brian Rix and broadcaster Sir Jimmy Saville, who said about his experience: "I went down as a boy and came up as a man."

One former pupil reports (to IMN) the school was camouflaged during the War, but a more likely explanation is that it may have appeared that way because building work went unfinished. Air-raid shelters were built at the front of the school, across the drive from the main entrance and the headmaster's office. The area between the drive and the shelters was developed as a rose garden.

The government was much concerned about gas attacks and everyone was issued with a carbon-filtered gas-mask which we carried with us everywhere. Many of us took to personalised decorating of the containers, but after a couple of years we left them at home or used them as sandwich boxes.(RJ)

There were regular air-raid practices when pupils with their gasmasks would file into the air-raid shelters. Fortunately the shelters were never used in earnest (EO). Doris Marks (1939 entry) recalls that as the school grew the shelters became too small and parents could opt for children to stay in the cloak-rooms instead.

As building work continued on the first floor, lessons were frequently interrupted by noise from above. Betty Oates recalls a builder going up a ladder outside her classroom window carrying a hod of bricks on which was painted "Graf Spee" – the first major enemy ship to be sunk in the war. (EO)

Miss Fell organised the adoption of a battleship and "We girls used to knit sea-boot stockings and jerseys. We liked to think there was a romance between her and the ship's captain!" (DOM). As the oiled wool was so heavy, jerseys were knitted in sections, e.g. a back or a front or a sleeve (KRG). A couple of boys joined the knitting group (probably because they fancied Miss Fell) and managed to produce stockings which didn't match in size (MPJ).

As part of their contribution to the war effort, which continued in fact for a couple of years after the war was over, volunteer pupils were dispatched to camps in the summer holidays for two weeks to work on farms. The girls went to Essex and to Somersham, near Huntingdon, picking fruit – mostly plums and apples (BF, EO, KG) whilst the boys went to Lincolnshire picking potatoes, singling turnips and stooking barley (WDB,RJ). Teachers Johnson and Quine even cooked at these camps and their elderberry and apple pie is fondly recalled by Roy Jackson, as are the boys' bicycle trips into Kirton Lindsey to replenish stocks of cider and currant buns.

Also working at these camps were German and Italian prisoners of war: "Content to be out of the firing lines and within sight of the land-girls" says Roy Jackson. One German prisoner reproached the Percy boys one day when they were fooling about, lobbing spuds at each other: "Unless you verk harder, you vill neffer vin zis vorr."

On the 1947 camp the girls were treated to a trip to Cambridge – "what a difference from our home area!" (DOM) It was at one of these camps that the girls happened to see Miss Olga Gray in her dressing gown and realised that her hair bun was fashioned from two long plaits (DOM).

Part of the school field was ploughed up and planted to food crops. Even after the War pupils went potato picking in the grounds in the late summer (JH). The first week of August 1948 was spent by thirty two older boys in the charge of Mr Horsfield and Mr Hanmer at a "Harvest Camp" at Blyborough near Gainsborough. They were billetted in the old rectory there and picked potatoes and peas and stooked corn (School Magazine 1949).

Percy Jackson's Hosts Evacuee Pupils

For four years (1940-44), boys of the **Riley High School in Hull** shared the school premises (SR). They had been evacuated from the East Riding and billetted with local families. Our later physics teacher, Alan Dixon, whilst a pupil at Maltby Grammar School, recalls a Saturday morning football fixture at Percy's against the Hull Boys in the winter of 1941-42. "We won rather easily" is his recollection.

A letter from the Hull school (24 August 1940) indicates an original plan for 167 boys: 55 from Bridlington, 67 from Selby and 40 "to be announced later". Norman Staveley, one of these Hull boys, explains (May 2005) that this was because they had already been previously evacuated in separate groups to Bridlington and Selby.

Other letters mention plans to billet the evacuees as: 33 in Askern, 14 in Burghwallis, 20 in Scawthorpe and 55 in the Barnsley Road area, which amounts to 122 pupils. Norman Staveley and a colleague, Charles Oxley, were billetted with the Manning family at "Mayfield" a mile from the water tower down Green Lane. He reports that, at the time of the May 1941 blitz, the glow from the flames of Hull could be seen from the Mannings' house – the A1 junction with Green Lane being quite a vantage point overlooking the lower Don Valley towards the Humber estuary (NSS).

Skellow boys remember they saw and heard the bombing over Sheffield and Rotherham and on one occasion the jettison of German bombs over Bentley (RJ). The roar of take-off and the cruising drone of the Halifax and Lancaster bombers from airfields around Doncaster (Finningley, Lindholme, Dunnington) became familiar to us all.

School records show the Hull boys were issued with 6381 dinner tickets in the autumn term of 1941, sufficient for around a hundred boys. In April 1943 they were recorded as 60 boys and four staff but by May 1944 it was expected that there would be only seven boys starting the autumn term and the redundancy of one of their staff, science teacher Mr Drinkall, was proposed. Judging by the thankyou letter from the Hull head (25 July 1944), it had been decided by the close of that summer term to repatriate all pupils and staff (SR/IMN).

There is one report that the Hull boys started and finished the school day at different times from the Piglets (BF).They occupied some of the first floor classrooms and used the lecture theatre as their assembly hall. Percy's pupils retained the use of the library, at the middle of the front wing on the first floor. The Hull boys had their own teachers and had a separate curriculum from Percy Jackson's (SR). This would explain Bill Bishop's observations "...they seemed to occupy some of the upstairs classrooms. For whatever reason, there seemed to be a strict segregation of the visitors from the residents" (WDB). Gwen (North) Oakland, who did not attend PJGS, has memories of "scuffles and scraps" breaking out between Hull boys and Percy's boys!

Riley High School masters at Percy's included: Dawson (chemistry), Drinkall (physics), Lucas (German), Forrest (English), Magee (maths) and Graystone, headmaster (NSS). The last seven Hull boys at Percy's are recorded as receiving their School Certificates in the prize-giving programme of 26 October 1944: W S Pawson, N S Staveley, F E Wilkinson, G L Burkitt, P C Garbutt, J C MacDonald and C W Oxley – although, being back in Hull, none of them attended the prize-giving.

School records show that Percy Jackson's also accommodated evacuee children from Kent, London and Middlesex although these pupils appear to have been incorporated into the main school. David Cranshaw recalls a Jewish boy from Germany, Johannes Schuster, who stayed for a few months before moving on with his family to the USA. Whilst English was a foreign tongue to him, he apparently got better marks in English Language than most of his classmates! (DC) Johannes never did understand why he was called "Fritz" by his schoolmates. (RJ)

As token examples of evacuee movements in Doncaster, here are two snippets from the *Doncaster Chronicle:*

Thursday 30 July 1944: "The number of evacuees received at Doncaster since last Saturday week has not been far short of three thousand."

Thursday 31 May 1945: "*London Evacuees Leave*: The first train under official auspices to take evacuees back to London from Doncaster and the surrounding areas will leave Doncaster on Tuesday. It will convey 400 mothers and children. Ninety of the party will be from the town area and the rest from the Rural District and from Adwick, Bentley, Goole and Thorne. Children who are unaccompanied will go about a week later. The Doncaster WVS has arranged an escort of ten for the party on Tuesday."

Many families of Percy pupils hosted evacuees, mostly children but also mothers with children. (IMN)

Expansion of School Premises

Completion of the original school premises appears to have been substantially delayed during the War, with the inherent shortages of both manpower and materials. It would appear that the school was planned to take an entry year of three classes, but from school year 1944-45 it was taking four classes, so overshooting its design capacity.
The *Doncaster Chronicle* of Thursday 26 July 1945 ran – in its Woodlands section:

> "*School Demands:* Owing to the large number of entrants in September, additional accommodation is being required for the Percy Jackson Grammar School." (IMN)

When they joined PJGS in September 1946, Richard Brooks and John Hudson recall attending first-year classes within the Adwick Park Junior school, commuting across to the main school for specialised facilities. In that year, 1946-47, two first-year classes, 1a and 1b, were housed in Adwick Park Junior School (JH). In that era the three classes of the fifth year were called 5L, 5S and 5P (Languages, Science, Practical).

Temporary Classrooms – 1948
The Wag of 47 reported that "*... the building was overfilled.*"

A U-shaped block of four classrooms with two cloakrooms was constructed of prefabricated concrete panels to the east of the gymnasium and began accommodating pupils from September 1948. This block was mainly to serve as form classrooms for first-year pupils (KC). By this time an entry year of four classes (about 120 pupils) had been established and the school roll number was nearly 650.

Writing in the School Magazine 1948-49, the head says "It is a pleasure to be able to record that these rooms have proved considerably more sightly, and pleasant to work in, than was expected when the word "prefabs" was first mentioned." A case of damning with faint praise?

Some twelve years later, the editorial of the Balkite 1960-61 expressed a more critical view, complaining: "Quite clearly therefore many of the difficulties experienced by the school have been caused by the Education Authority's insistence on developing the school too quickly" and decried the "prefabricated rooms which still disfigure the rear of the school."

New Science Block – 1954

Situated across the boys' playground to the north of the main building, the new two-storey L-shaped block comprised two chemistry labs and a preparation room on the ground floor and two biology labs and a preparation room on the first floor. The adjoining wing had four general purpose classrooms downstairs and two domestic science rooms on the first floor, cooking and handicraft, together with associated store rooms.(KC)

From the autumn term of 1954 the school started to receive five entry forms and included pupils from a slightly wider area which included the south Wakefield district (South Elmsall, Upton) and the Smeaton area of the North Riding (FJA). Carol (Pearson) Edgar recalls that she started in September 1954 in a five-class first-year and that her home form-room was the end one on the ground floor of the new block. The new block was officially opened on the 10 February 1955 (School Magazine 1954-55).

1963-68 Buildings for the New Comprehensive

The proposed comprehensive school would need to house roughly double the number of pupils and construction of premises to accommodate the increased population commenced in 1963. It attracted comment in the school magazine The Balkite 1963-64:

> I believe that the building, which is made of corrugated chewing gum, is to be a jam butty factory, as they have now struck butty ore under the coal at Brodsworth pit.
>
> J. Moorley 4A

> Unfortunately it has been erected where the school hockey pitches used to be and, because of the 'fantastic' shooting accuracy of the girls, the whole building may begin to roll about on the hundreds of stray hockey balls.
>
> A. Harland 4A

The first sixth form of The Adwick School was provided with its own block about eighty metres behind the metalwork room and near the old prefab building. It is reported as being a welcome facility — "quite sumptuous". Downstairs were cloakrooms and a sixth form common room with soft furnishings. Upstairs there were a couple of classrooms, a library and an office for the head of the sixth form, who initially was Mr Herbert Mayman. Bob Dunkley (1964-69) reports that the covered walkway from near the corner of the metalwork room to this block was paid for by funds raised by the new sixth form.

In an echo of 1946-47, when first-formers commuted across the road to and from Adwick Primary School, in 1967-68 the lower sixth were accommodated with their opposite numbers across the road in Adwick High School in preparation for the conversion to the comprehensive in August 1968.

Evolution of the School Roll

Pupils: 1939 – 85   1945 – 450   1948 – 650

            1955 – 700   1960 – 860   1962 – 890

Staff :   1939 – 5   1945 – 22   1955 – 33   1961 – 40   1966 – 41

Headmasters

Mr Ronald Field 1939-1945 (KC)
" More an emergency ward than a grammar school."

David Cranshaw recalls Mr Field as a dapper gentleman with a pencil moustache. Mollie Peet remembers him as a wonderful teacher with a kindly attitude towards pupils. She felt he chose teachers of a similar disposition which all made for a happy school environment – "a unique ethos", she reports. By comparison, she felt the next headmaster, Mr Elliott, was rather severe.

One has to wonder what Mr Field's reflections were on leaving Percy's at the end of 1944. He had originally been appointed to open, manage and build up a shining new grammar school. His plans were immediately shattered, almost literally, by the bombshell of World War II. The building itself was not quite finished, perhaps half of his hand-picked male teachers were drafted into military service and he had to find replacements from a probably less able pool – including bringing back teachers from retirement.

Far from rushing to finish the building, efforts were diverted to constructing air raid shelters and to training pupils and staff in gasmask and evacuation drill. With incomplete premises and a shortage of staff he was struggling to build up the roll number, when someone had the bright idea of grafting on the Hull school with its own staff and a separate curriculum. And at some point through this turbulence, he tragically loses the the school caretaker!

Mr Field deserved a medal simply for retaining his sanity. The School Records show he at least received a very warm letter of appreciation (25 July 1944) from the Hull school's head, Mr F Walker, after their boys had returned home. Mr Field must have drawn some satisfaction from the knowledge that he was leaving a school "ready and running" for the next head.

At a personal level, Mr Field was also caring for his wife – a charming lady - who suffered from a progressively debilitating disease, probably multiple sclerosis (RJ).

Mr Cecil Elliott ("Chas") 1945 – 1966. (JH)

Mr Elliott, known affectionately as "Chas" or "Charley", became the school's second headteacher in September 1945. Immediately before, he was Head of History at Goole Grammar School and earlier in his career had taught at Wigton Grammar School. In Wigton he met his wife Nell who was daughter of a local policeman. Mr Elliott came from the mining area of Northumberland. He went to Ashington Grammar School and was a graduate of Durham University. Mr and Mrs Elliott did not have any family and during his time at PJGS they lived on Crabgate Drive, Skellow. After retirement in 1966, they moved to Papcastle near Cockermouth in Cumbria where Mrs Elliott died in the late 1990s and Mr Elliott in 2002 at the age of 96.

Mr Elliott was a tall, distinguished-looking man with grey-blue piercing eyes. On first meeting he could appear quite severe but his somewhat stern exterior belied an inner warmth and sense of humour. He was strict but fair and on occasion was moved to reach for the cane from his cupboard. He always wanted the best for his staff and pupils and led from the front, setting very high standards. As one former pupil put it "We were taught in a humane and even entertaining way. We received a broad and rounded education and were encouraged to stretch ourselves into other fields." Mr Elliott joined in many school activities and is fondly remembered and admired for taking part in drama productions, turning out as left-back in the annual Staff v School First XI Soccer match and singing bass with the Senior Choir. Throughout his time at PJGS and into retirement Mr Elliott maintained a keen interest in the lives and careers of former pupils and he and Mrs Elliott gave a warm welcome to anyone visiting them in Papcastle. In that more relaxed setting he would even address 'boys' by Christian name rather than by surname as in their school days.

Many pupils will echo the sentiments of one former pupil (AL) who, on hearing about Mr. Elliott's death, said "We owe him a lot and have a lot to thank him for". A former member of staff (GC) said "The first headmaster I had and he was the kindest, the most understanding and, in short, the best".

Chas turns out to be one of the longest serving members of staff. On 22 July 1966 he entered in the log book "Last day of school session, after 21 years service as Head Master." (SR/IMN).

Mr F John Atherfold 1966-1968

Mr Atherfold was head of the Grammar School during its final two years and continued as head of the comprehensive, Adwick School, until his retirement in July 1988.

John Atherfold was a mathematics graduate who, after a short spell in the aircraft industry, turned to teaching. He experienced some of the first comprehensives in the country, became head of mathematics at Tulse Hill School and then Deputy Head of Nicholas Chamberlaine Comprehensive School, the first comprehensive in Warwickshire, before being appointed Head at Percy Jackson's at the age of 34.

The change to comprehensive had already been decided when he took over and he was determined to keep alive the academic traditions of grammar schools. After the final entry for PJGS in the school log book, Mr Atherfold wrote *"May the best of its achievements live on in the new school."* (SR)

He reports (private communication: 16 Oct 2004) that academic results improved considerably from 1968 onwards and that greater emphasis was given to the teaching of science subjects without altering the provision of French (by then the first foreign language), German and Latin.

He mentions an odd little coincidence: the tie of his old school, Bishopshalt, Hillingdon, was identical to that of Percy Jackson's — so he wears a Percy's tie to his old school reunions!

Senior Masters and Mistresses

Senior Mistresses
Miss Hellena Todd 1939-1942   Miss Evelyn Banks 1942-1949
Miss D J Dent 1949-1965   Mrs Sheila Wood 1965-1968

Senior Masters
Mr V Milson: From the school's opening in 1939, before being drafted into

the services. Returned briefly Jan-Aug 1945 (following war service) and was acting Head for the interregnum between Mr Field and Mr Elliott.

Mr L C Johnson: Acting Senior Master 1940-44 (during Mr Milson's absence)

Mr Bill Quine: Acting Senior Master briefly from Mr Johnson's departure until the arrival of Mr Cunnington.

Mr W J Cunnington 1945-1964 (died in service)

In a tribute, Mr Elliott recorded: "… he was one of the most selfless men….his dedication to work inspired respect. A man of the highest integrity and principle, he set an example which all could follow." (SM 1963-64.)

Mr H Mayman 1964-1968

The "**High Trinity**" referred to by the Wag of 1947, if you have not realised, consisted of the Headmaster, the Senior Mistress and the Senior Master, who fronted the staff platform at morning assembly.

The School Rules (KC)

These were brief yet comprehensive:

> 1) Walk on the left side of the corridor.
> 2) At all times act with due consideration for others.

Rule One was the basic traffic law, essential between lessons as pupils moved between classsrooms and specialised facilities. "Walk" carried a specific significance in that it prohibited running – and was a source of many penalties.

Rule Two supposed a certain level of morality, perhaps beyond the grasp of exuberant eleven- to thirteen-year olds, but the penalties earned on infringement of this "catch-all" rule served as a useful form of improvement. On occasion Mr Field felt he had to explain during morning "notices" that it was not appropriate to be openly affectionate in public. It was not "suitable" for girls and boys to be seen holding hands or with arms around each other (KRG). Arguably a case of infringing Rule 2 : insufficient consideration for others.

Policing was provided by teachers, prefects and sub-prefects. Detentions could only be imposed by teachers and the main penalties consisted of "lines" or writing an essay related – or not – to one's misdemeanour. "Lines" meant writing out repetitively, say fifty or a hundred times or more, a statement reminding one of one's crime or simply copying out one or both of the School Rules. For the worst crimes, of course, boys could be caned by the head and this continued through into Mr Atherfold's time. The first head, Mr Field, however did not keep a cane and did not permit corporal punishment (MPJ).

There seemed to be a third, unwritten rule, which could perhaps be regarded as an extension of Rule Two. This was applied more strictly by some teachers than others and might be envisaged as "Outside school hours you will behave only in a manner which reflects well on the School." Depending on interpretation, this would prohibit shouting, fighting, scuffling and dropping litter in the street, and require due acknowledgement of staff outside school hours. In the view of some teachers this rule required that boys should raise their caps to staff in town, not a gesture that many miners' sons could readily accommodate.

School Houses

Initially there were only three school houses – red, green and black (EO). As the number of pupils built up, four houses were established: **Lane** (greens) and **Jackson** (yellows), named after West Riding aldermen, **Washington** (reds), after the Washington family, and **Markham** (blues), a prominent family of mine-owners in the region (KC). Or, as the Wag of 1947 recorded in the School Magazine:

> *"And the tribes are united under four roofs, namely, Jack's House, the Washhouse, the Roadhouse and the House of the Blue Pencil."*

David Cranshaw, who joined the third form in 1939, reports (Dec 2004) that he was the first captain of the boys' Blue Pencil err… Markham house, Cyril Knight captain of Washington, John Perry captain of Lane and Tom Cox captain of Jackson. In the very early days David and Cyril helped to run the school Tuck Shop, selling confectionery to pupils, but this fell an early casualty to wartime with the rationing of sugar.

School Uniform

Originally, children from other schools – viz mainly secondary modern - would refer to us as "**Percies**" which carried undertones of both snob and sissy - or worse! This together with our uniform - especially the distinctive cap for the boys - could make life a bit of a challenge in one's home village, particularly when we were so small in numbers (DM). In the late forties, however, as we grew in number and in confidence, the popular image adjusted to something more beastly. We became known as "**Percy's Piglets**".

Boys' Uniform: Malcolm Palmer

The male version of school uniform consisted of a grey blazer or jacket, which was, unfortunately, capable of a great many subtle variations. The objective of any school uniform, of course, is to give some measure of uniformity, thus preventing the rich/poor division from surfacing in the classroom environment. And to some extent, of course, this was achieved, but the tell-tale sewn-on badge on the breast-pocket of the cheap jacket bought on Donny market quickly set it aside from the 'official item' purchased from the relatively snooty clothiers – John Manners Ltd, at 1 & 2 Market Place in Doncaster.

A grey shirt, as school photos will reveal, often had a less-than-perfect collar (not unusual in those pre-polyester days) but worst of all was *the tie*. This slender item, black, with diagonal red and green stripes managed to droop into half one's meals and after a couple of washings soon resembled a piece of chewed string. A further contributory factor was that the tie was normally the second point of contact – as in violent yanking – in playground scuffles. The first point of contact being to grab and throw away your adversary's school cap.

The whole *ensemble* was complemented by the obligatory school cap, an almost invariably too-small, plain black job with a little badge, inviting robbery by the village lads whenever smaller 'Piglets' arrived in their home environment. One school cap remained for over six months at the very top of an immensely high pylon which carried the buckets of colliery waste at Bullcroft Main. Its owner was inordinately proud of having climbed up and put it there, despite catching hell from his mother.

For boys and for girls the wearing of indoor shoes – black plimsolls - was obligatory.

The **original boys' cap** was a more ornate article. Basically black, it had a red median band around it and a green segment at the front, bearing the badge.(RJ) It seems to have disappeared – along with other parts of the uniform - with the introduction of clothing coupons during the war and after rationing it was replaced with a plain black cap with badge.

In 1943 the costs, in shillings (s) and pence (d), of uniform items were: (SR/IMN)

Blazer	**19s 0d**	**Cap**	**3s 3d**	**Gym shoes**	**1s 9d**
Short trousers	**9s 0d**	**Tie**	**2s 3d**	**Pullover**	**7s 6d**
Football shirt	**3s 6d**	**Football Stockings 2s 0d**			

Total: £2-8s-3d or in decimal currency about £2.41.

By 1950 a school blazer cost about 30 shillings (£1.50). (KC)

By 1959 a blazer cost around 60/-d (60 shillings or £3.00) and a school tie was 6/11d (nearly 35 pence) (JKR).

From about 1954 items of uniform were also available from Burras Peake Ltd in Carcroft. From 1958 Drury & Co, Printing Office Street, Doncaster were also stockists of uniform, from 1962 Doncaster Co-op Society at the Emporium and from 1963 Mimi's of Netherhall Road, Doncaster. (Adverts in School Magazines)

Girls' Uniform

The Original Uniform: Kathleen Gibson Pumfrey.

When the school first opened, the girls' uniform was not available to buy from any shop. A "tailor" came to school during the first term and girls were given an appointment. Their mothers were also expected to attend. Measuring took place in the medical room, next to the senior mistress's room. Measurements were generous – to allow for growth. The uniform was eventually delivered to school.

The pleated skirt was called a "kilt". Made of pale grey gaberdine it buttoned onto a cotton bodice. Most of us had tucks taken into the bodice and buttons raised. The kilt could therefore be lengthened as needed. Mine lasted me all the five years I attended PJGS!

Made of a fabric called "Tobralco", the short-sleeved white blouses, since they could not be tucked into the kilt, were finished at the waist with a band which buttoned at the front. A matching band finished off the sleeves. In cold weather we were allowed to wear a long-sleeved pale grey jumper, instead of the blouse, but it had to have a turn-down collar which could accommodate the school tie. In later years a v-necked jumper worn over the blouse was permitted, so showing the tie.

The blazer was of grey flannel. Socks were regulation grey wool knee socks for winter. Grey lisle stockings were allowed after the third form. The hat was a broad-brimmed black velour with the school badge on the front of the hatband, which was horizontally striped in the school colours.

The summer uniform was an emerald green linen dress with white collar and cuffs, which were designed to be removed for washing. Most of us sewed on clean starched collar and cuffs at mid-week. Short white socks were worn in summer.

The gym dress was an all-in-one dress and shorts in a light green, which was excellent in the gym but miserably cold on the hockey field. We were not allowed to wear a vest underneath them. All girls had to wear indoor shoes, which were black "ward" shoes as worn by nurses in hospital. They were very light, made of soft leather and fastened over with a single strap which buttoned at the side. However, due to wartime rationing this rule was later relaxed and plimsolls could be worn (DOM).

In Miss Todd's time it was a crime to attend school in less than perfect uniform and a mark on one's kilt was punished by an order mark known as a "debit".

By the time Mollie Peet joined in 1942, uniform headwear was not required she says. Because of rationing and the clothing coupon system schools could not enforce the purchase of uniform. Mollie further reports "It was only in about 1945 when some of us girls decided it would be cool to wear black berets; so we approached "Fanny" Banks (senior mistress) and put this proposition to her. She went along with it, and agreed that sixth form girls should be allowed to wear black berets ornamented by a school badge. We wore them, of course, at an angle hardly imagined by Fanny – but it kept us happy."

The Modern Version: Anne Limbert Stidwell
It was an established fact that the girls were more smartly dressed than the boys **plus** we had separate uniforms for winter and for summer!

The winter uniform was a grey skirt - adapted as much as we dared as we became more aware of fashion - with a white long-sleeved blouse and the standard black tie with its green and red diagonal stripes. Outdoors, we wore navy blue garberdine macs. The summer uniform was a green and white candy-striped dress. Initially this was ordered from school and then mothers, such as mine, would decide that it could be made at home. The style was not at all attractive and one imagines the design was intended to fit all shapes and sizes.

For all-year wear we had grey blazers with the school badge on the left-hand breast pocket and white ankle socks were worn. Grey knee socks were permitted, but that mostly applied to the first form. After many requests, we were allowed to wear 30 denier brown nylon stockings when we were in the Senior School. It took a long time for the white tide marks left by the ankle socks to fade. Headwear was originally (in the early 40s) a black velour hat with a red and green band but this was displaced in the mid 40s by a black beret bearing the school badge. On reaching the Sixth Form we were privileged to wear emerald green berets! Wearing the beret was obligatory and if – by wearing any other headdress - one failed to conform, the ultimate punishment was to stand at the front of school assembly wearing the offending item!

The most remarkable piece of girls' uniform was the light green cotton gym dress. It was one piece - blouse and pleated shorts - and was very difficult to put on and to take off. We were measured for these by the headmistress. It was always chests that were measured and busts were never mentioned! Much of our time in needlework was spent in making green cotton knickers to wear under the gym dresses. This remains most firmly impressed on one's memory - both the sewing and the wearing. When these green creations split or wore out we were allowed to wear shop bought ones in navy or grey ETB (**E**lastic **T**op and **B**ottom!).

In needlework class we also made aprons and caps for wearing in domestic science lessons. Much more civilized was our hockey kit - pleated grey shorts, white shirts and bright red knee socks!

First Day At School

Starting at Percy's was a big event for most families. Joy Cuffling (L VI) in the 1949-50 Magazine likens it to bereavement, when a mother realizes her treasure has gone and his room is empty:

> "She turned and went back downstairs where her husband was absorbed in his newspaper. Sitting down she sniffed "Oh, John, isn't it lonely without him?" "Now, don't take on so" he said, clumsily attempting comfort "You'll soon get used to it – it was high time he went to school , and anyway, he'll be home by dinnertime."

CHAPTER 2

School Traditions

"Pioneers" (DC)

During Mr Field's headship, the first morning assembly of each new term always included hymn 304 from the schools' enlarged edition of "Songs of Praise". Written by Walt Whitman, this was known as "Pioneers" and the first verse ran:

> All the past we leave behind:
> We take up the task eternal, and the burden, and the lesson,
> Conquering, holding, daring, venturing, so we go the unknown ways,
> Pioneers! O Pioneers!

The entrants of those first years, the War years, were indeed the school's pioneers.

Annual Prize-Giving – "Speech Day"

The school's first Speech Day was on 12 December 1940, presided over by Mr A L Binns, Director of Education, West Riding County Council. Subsequent prize-givings were usually held in early November.(SR) In 1946 there were two *"Annual"* prize-givings – on the 14 March and on the 7 November. The March 1946 programme appears to have commemorated achievements in academic year 1944-45, the last year of the War.

The pattern was that the Headmaster gave his annual report and dignitaries were wheeled in to preside over the prize-giving, to praise our achievements and to exhort us to greater things. At the 4 November 1948 prize-giving, guest of honour Professor Potter, reviewing Doncaster's history pointed out "The West Riding, as large as some sovereign states, is a place to be proud of." He went on to praise the contribution of grammar schools: "Their war record has shown what the grammar schools of this country can do. Without trained brains we could not have succeeded......The country rightly holds its grammar schools in esteem, passing on - as they do – the precious heritage of our western civilisation." (SM 1948-49).

Addressing us on the 11 November 1949, the Rt Hon the Earl of Halifax referred to Sir Percy Jackson "as a typical son of the West Riding" and urged us to "let him be your example of citizenship". With "kindly humour" he went on to advise "Honestly form your judgement and mean to do good to your country. Your school tradition will then surely grow." (SM 1949-50).

On the 17 November 1950 in his headmaster's report Mr Elliot, referring to the development of pupils, mentioned: "...we can, where necessary, apply extra discipline so that habitual idleness or carelessness is not allowed to take root." He also said that examinations were not the whole point of school life "whose purpose is much wider and deeper." Our guest of honour was Sir Ronald Matthews who said that education required both good teachers and good pupils: "The material on which they have to work must be good also. The jockey cannot come away without a good horse; there must be cooperation between child and staff."

Guest of honour, Professor E B Castle, at the November 6th prize-giving of 1952 had this advice for pupils leaving school: "Try so to live that you can always say that now is the best time of your life."

In his headmaster's report to the prize-giving on 5th November 1953 Mr

Elliott was concerned at the number of boys engaged in part-time work. He questioned whether this could affect their school work and their participation in extra-curricular activities. At the same event Alderman T Tomlinson BEM quoted a remark made by Sir Percy Jackson: "We are living in an age of silent revolution – in thought." In encouraging pupils to work hard Ald Tomlinson urged us to remember "that the virtue lay in the struggle and not the prize."

On the 3rd November 1955 Mr Elliott was saying that ability needed to be accompanied by perseverance and hard work, with a resolve to do one's best. In other words "character as well as ability". At the 1956 prize-giving, he continued his theme of school providing a more rounded education "preparing pupils for living and not just a livelihood." On this occasion, guest of honour Professor Brynmor Jones asked parents to consider that "the waste in a teacher's workshop are the lives of men." Addressing pupils, he said he wouldn't give them advice since "the wise don't need it and fools won't take it." Nevertheless, he exhorted them to work hard. (SM 1956-57)

At the 1957 Speech Day, despite good A-level results, Mr Elliott was concerned at the reduced number, especially of boys, entering the sixth form. Guest of honour Professor H C Dent urged parents and pupils to recognise the value of staying on in the sixth form: "years which could never be made up later in life." In truth, at this time good wages were being paid to school leavers and staying on was seen as making a financial sacrifice. In this vein, the editorial of the 1960-61 Balkite noted "Full employment has removed the incentive to acquire good qualifications when well-paid jobs can be obtained without them."

By the 1958 Speech Day, the head's worst fears had been averted, as a record forty pupils entered the Lower Sixth. Guest of honour Professor W Walsh made the point that intelligence combined with education meant that we were not mere "creatures of circumstances or helpless lackeys of fate."

In 1959 "Chas" again pleaded for more pupils to stay on in the Sixth Form, particularly in view of the country's desperate shortage of teachers and technologists. This view was supported by guest of honour Professor W R

Niblett who referred to the high proportion of scientists and technologists in other countries. In addition to personal ambitions and achievement, he stressed that friendliness and cooperation were important qualities in an individual.

School year 1960-61 was Percy Jackson's "coming of age" and the headmaster's report in November 1960 reflected on the first twentyone years of its history. In Lady Littlewood, president of the Professional Women's Clubs, the school welcomed its first female speaker. She referred to the "wastage incurred by so many women refusing to take advantage of their education and regarding a career as a stop-gap between school and marriage." On 7th November 1963, the school welcomed a second female guest of honour, Miss Joyce Bloxham, Tutor of Women Students at Leeds University.

Building Tradition (KC)

By the late 1940s and early 50s one detects a thread in Speech Days and School Magazine comments concerning a lack of "tradition" at the Percy Jackson Grammar School. The topic must have been exercising the minds of school governors and senior staff. But how can a new institution have instant traditions? Furthermore, they must have been comparing PJGS with established grammar schools, some of which had over a hundred years of history, and most of them were either boarding schools or were located in towns, necessitating very little daily travel for their pupils.

This new school was located in a village and drew its pupils from quite a spread of other villages on the northern side of Doncaster. So firstly there was a question of cohesion amongst the school community. Secondly, except for the minority who lived in Woodlands and Adwick-le-Street, pupils faced a few miles cycling or a bus trip to and from school. School special buses collected and delivered pupils free of charge, but if one missed the "special" the journey home would take longer. It might entail more than one bus trip and would have to be paid for. This must surely have affected pupils' attitudes to extra-curricular activities.

And thirdly, we nearly all came from families which had no experience of school tradition. One can appreciate why the school governors were concerned about the issue. They may not have realised it, but despite the many obstacles, the school was indeed developing its own traditions, as I hope this *History* demonstrates: the German connection, the choirs, the dining hall, the lively societies and clubs, the inter-house cross-country, Cricket Week, the school plays, school travel and the continuing story in the School Magazine, to mention just a few.

School Magazine

Initially, the magazine was a few typed sheets reproduced by stencil-copy. The first printed edition seems to have appeared in December 1946, since the following issue of December 1947 was titled as No.2. In this issue the editor wrote "It is hoped that the magazine may in future become a twice-yearly publication." This hope appears not to have been realised and from 1949 it was published annually in July, at the end of the school year.

The *"School Magazine"*, or *"The Balkite"* as it came to be called for the last nine years of the school's life, was - and remains − an illuminating record of Percy's academic, sporting and social activities. The trauma of the name change is reflected in the title of the final *"School Magazine"* which was erroneously dated 1959-60 but actually was 1958-59! The first *"Balkite"* was 1959-60 and its name relates of course to the school's location bewteen the two "balks" - Windmill and Tenter. In the 1968 Balkite, headmaster Mr Atherfold notes that there was no issue of the magazine in school year 1966/67.

As well as providing records of school events and sporting achievements, the School Magazine was an outlet for aspiring poets and writers.

> **So bin ich selig** (third verse only)
> Jetzt aber, als ich mehr verstehe,
> Und die weite Welt ganz anders sehe,
> Ist es wieder möglich ruhig zu sein,
> Denn Liebe und Freundschaft nenne ich mein.
>
> Tony Waddoups U VI, School Magazine 1955-56.

And I am blessed

And now, as my understanding grows,

I see the world quite differently.

Tempered are my sorrows

Since love and friendship belong to me.

Translation: KC.

Advertising helped to defray production costs and initially most advertisements were placed by local retailers, predominantly from Woodlands. Later some Doncaster shops, especially clothiers, placed advertisements and then came the big banks and the National Coal Board with promises of careers. Some features from the National Coal Board advertisements:

1956 : Modern Coalmining is very largely a new industry.

1957:   To meet the increasing demands for coal, vast schemes of reconstruction and expansion are being undertaken…

1958 : A career for young men that carries responsibility.

1959:   Britain's prosperity depends on power.

1960:   The bulk of this energy must, for many generations, continue to come from coal.

1961:   It is possible to earn a four-figure salary by the age of thirty.

1964:   Room at the Top with a Chance to Change Things.

1968:   Make the most of your 'O' and 'A' levels. Put them into Coal!

Alas, we now know what happened to the coal mining industry in the region.

By 1964 even Barclays Bank was starting to feel the impact of girl power. Their advertisement was framed under two headings:

"For ambitious young men."

"And there's scope for girls as well."

I leave it to campaign-hardened feminists to explain any significance in the forms of labelling. The same advertisement went on to promise *"Incidentally, a girl who marries after five years' service with the Bank qualifies for a gratuity."* How things have changed!

The School Magazine along with the School Records constitute the major written resources for this *History*.

Morning Assembly

The Wag of 47 records:

> *"And it is ordained that, at the first sounding of the timbrel all tribes and clans and sects shall congregate together that they may be presided over by the High Trinity, which doth govern all things, from the appointing of the elders, yea, until the sounding of the timbrel."*

After morning registration in their "home" classrooms, each class made its way to the school hall for Assembly. Prefects supervised the alignment of classes in the hall: first year at the front through to fifth year at the back. In the early years, when there were fewer pupils, everyone had a chair but as the school neared full complement forms 1 to 5 had to sit on the floor: girls on the left and boys on the right, and sixth formers along each side – with chairs!

Teachers then assembled on the stage to await the entrance of the headmaster and senior mistress. Headmaster would lead a prayer and a hymn and then instruct the school to "Sit" before making the day's announcements. Dennis Smith (1939) and Mollie Paver (1940) recall that in the early years, once each week a member of staff would introduce and play a record of a piece of classical music. Mollie Peet believes this was the idea of Mr Field.

At the end of assembly it was "Stand" whilst the head and teachers left the stage. Classes then filed out of the hall under the supervision of prefects to assume their daily schedule. The Wag of 47 has it that:

> *"And at the second sounding of the timbrel, all clans and tribes shall disperse to the religion for which each is claimed, yea, verily to the B1 sect or the D1 sect, or the sect of many tongues.*
> *And some shall sport and play and exercise themselves with stick and spheres and things: the night rakes combatting those from the laundry.*
> *And a few shall practise the mystic arts of messing with pottage and spinning yarns. And others shall exercise their vocal chords, imitating the sweet music which heralded the arrival of Fritz and drowning the sound of the timbrel."*

By 1956, as the school roll expanded, the numbers for assembly became too large for the hall and a separate assembly – held in the gymnasium - for the five classes of the first year (150 young souls) was inaugurated.

School Meals

A war-time grace, recalled by Roy Jackson:

> "For this our food… the meat, the gravy,
> We thank thee Lord …and the Merchant Navy."

With slightly less grace:

> "For what we are about to receive, may the Lord make us truly thankful.
> For Christ's sake – sit down!"
>
> Attributed to Mr Pilsworth (Jo Huddleston)

The Wag of 47 had this to say:

> *"And the sounding of the timbrel shall announce the occasion of feasting, yea, of great jubilation, which shall be accompanied by shouting and appetising odours.*
>
> *And an elder shall be there and a chief, and he shall bless the food and receive the tithes.*
>
> *And they shall feed on legumes and spheres of lepidoptera and unleavened bread★.*
>
> *Then they shall wander ad lib in the precincts among the trees till the time is passed, yea, till the sounding of the timbrel"*

The quality of the meals – midday lunch - in the dining hall was much appreciated from the beginning (WDB, MH). Although we never went hungry at home during the war, rationing meant that meals were a bit monotonous

---

★Alluding to mothball sago pudding with shortbread biscuit.

and some items of diet were a bit thin on the ground. The good and inexpensive school lunches were probably a big help to our families. (RJ)

In 1940 a dinner ticket cost 9d, although the Hull boys were subsidised and paid only 6^1/$_2$d (SR/IMN) - pronounced "sixpence hayp'ny". Each table of eight had a "server" and deputy server appointed from the more senior pupils – later they would be chosen from prefects and sub-prefects.

Originally, the servers collected tureens from the serving hatch and took them to their tables, where they were politely passed around, each pupil serving themself (KRG). In the late 40s the servers collected meals, two at a time, from the kitchen counter and delivered them to their table. At the fourth, last trip, hoping for a good helping, a bold server would whisper to the kitchen lady "Er…, this one is for me."(JH)

The system changed slightly in the 1950s when the servers collected whole dishes from the kitchen counter. The duty - or challenge - of the server then became to divide each dish fairly amongst the pupils at the table, serving him/herself last (KC).

"Dinner tickets" for the week were purchased each Monday morning from one's form teacher. Pupils had to sign them on the back and write on their form number. Before lunch we queued in the corridor outside the dining hall and as we entered tickets were collected by the prefects on dinner duty. In the dining hall boys and girls were segregated, no doubt to shelter the girls from the boys' poor table habits. Well, it's very hard to restrain a hungry young lad.

Not surprisingly, some menus were more popular than others, though Roy Jackson recalls that no matter what was on the menu "somebody on the table of eight would always clear the lot". He also claims that the domestic science teacher of the early 40s (Miss Johnson) had an undue influence on menu design "with her predilection for haricot beans in white sauce - which would have been better employed by a wallpaper hanger". In the 1950s the macaroni cheese pie was not highly regarded by the girls, which meant that the boys got copious second helpings. Amongst the boys, sago ("mothballs" or "frogspawn") and semolina puddings got a mixed reception. About a quarter of them refused to eat "such slime" and left the dining hall early, taking the accompanying shortbread biscuit in their pocket to eat in the playground – the famous "Pocket Pudding"(KC). Some retain fond memories of the heavier sponge or suet puddings – "stodges" - accompanied by custard or over-sweet treacle. (RJ)

As the five-year intake worked its way up through the school, the dining hall became too small and by 1958 a second sitting for lunch was installed. In 1967 a third sitting was introduced at the beginning of the new school year. This was all too much for Miss Brown, the Kitchen Supervisor, and she resigned before the end of September.

Ode to School Dinners

The war-like dance with solemn grace begins
With silent awe they greet the lofty hall;
In ordered lines of mystic length
While brawny guards stand firmly by,
To choose their victim innocent and meek,
Its pleas for mercy are mere fruitless cries,
'They hurl him midst the hostile tribes.
They bow with reverence and holy joy,
And when at last they struggle to their feet
They see the sacrificial altars long,
Whereon the juicy offering will soon appear.
The ringing bell invokes a deadly hush
As with their bowed heads the ritual ends.
They now await the succulent new joint
As portals of the inmost sanctuary are opened wide,
Revealing lamb or beef or pork, perhaps,
Or had we better say… just meat

J.Turner LVI – School magazine "The Balkite" 1961-62

Boys' Lunchtime Sports

After lunch, boys would indulge in informal sports "till the sounding of the timbrel". In the 40s and 50s one of these was **Mass Soccer** on the boys' playground using a small ball, often a tennis ball. One goal was the space between drainpipes on the toilet wall and the other was the gap in the kerb on the north side of the asphalt, reinforced perhaps with a couple of jumpers or blazers. There were no fixed playing positions, apart from having two sides with a goalkeeper at each end, and very few rules. Any number of boys could join in and nobody was turned away. There were often up to fifty on the "pitch". Of course, when the ball went onto the roof of the boys' cloak-rooms, or even over into the quadrangle, some wild spirit would always "scrim" up a drainpipe to retrieve it. (RJ).

An alternative soccer game was sometimes played on the access drive behind the kitchen, the novel features being that there were no teams and only a single, narrow goal between a kitchen drain and a downpipe. Anyone wishing to strike had to stop someone else's shot first. The limited space meant that only up to about twenty lads could play, but it was a fast and furious game. As in the mass game, scores were not kept: taking part was the important thing. (KC)

In better weather, mainly in the summer term, inpromptu forms of cricket were played as well as "ball throwing", which took two forms: a) throwing a hard ball fast and straight to a catcher who would return it randomly to another catcher and b) throwing the ball to maximum vertical height and "catch as catch can" when it descended. Great heights and great catches were applauded. (KC)

Also in the better weather some faux gymnastics took place after lunch: leapfrog, handsprings, cartwheels and the like. Horse vaulting or husky-fusky sometimes resulted in collapse and then all the gang would spontaneously join in, diving onto the fallen heap. "*Heaps*" it was called and might have involved twenty bodies. Lord knows why we did it – but it seemed fun at the time! (KC)

Global Warming

We all remember winters being very hard in those days: delayed buses, trudging through the snow to school, daring onto iced ponds, rolling up a giant ball and throwing snowballs – enthusiastically or aggressively (that would only have been the boys, of course!). (KC)

On a very frosty day, especially if there had previously been rain or snow, early arrivers would start an ice slide across the tarmac of the boys' playground and the more people used it the glossier and the longer it got. By the first timbrel a slide might have reached 50 feet (15 metres) or more in length and would be extremely fast, not to mention dangerous. The occasional sprained or broken limb was a seasonal hazard. The anticipation through the early lessons was to use the slide again in morning break or at lunchtime. (RJ)

Interestingly, according to data from the Climate Research Unit, University of East Anglia, there was a period of relative **global cooling** from 1940 to 1965. (Sunday Telegraph, 9 April 2006).

School Buses

The Wag of 47 says it all really:

> *"And each shall to his allotted task , till the final timbrel shall sound, yea, till the end of the day.*
>
> *And then shall each return to his clan, to the clan of Bentley and the clan of Skellow and the clan of Sprotborough.*
>
> *And there shall be chariots there, and coaches, and they shall be called "Special" chariots.*
>
> *And the elders shall travel in the first chariot – which is usually the last – and people of all tribes shall journey in the chariots, yea, even to Skellow and Askern and the City of the Donne.*
>
> *Those only shall remain from the Blue Pencil House, and the House that Jack Built, who combat each other with spheres and sticks and things.*
>
> *Woe be on the heads of those who incur the displeasure of the High Trinity and the Elders, for they shall remain in the building till the appointed hour."*
>
> (Viz: in detention)

Annual Boys' Cross-Country Race

Starting in 1954, at the end of the spring term each year all boys – some 300 be-shorted souls – were pitched out for the annual Inter-house Cross-country.

One needed a cast-iron excuse or a limb in plaster to get out of this event, but there were always a few try-ons! Which was the greater indignity – running a pathetic three miles or pleading for exemption? Character-building had a definite place on Mr Cockroft's agenda! Finishing up the home straight (from Adwick village to the gym), where all the spectators were girls – apart from the few lads with plaster casts - carried its own reward. (KC)

Skiving from Cross-Country Runs (boys)

Cross-country runs were a regular feature of boys' sports through the winter. Various shortcuts were established. An early one was to loiter for 15 to 20 minutes at the air raid shelter at the top of Tenter Balk Lane and then to amble down the backs of the houses to join the genuine runners as they entered Adwick village towards the end of the run (JH).

A slight variant of this route was favoured by the "Daisy Pickers", the name given by Mr Cockroft to a group of arts sixthformers circa 1955 who were *not athletically gifted* (DNP). Other ruses involved a 'rest' at pubs such as the Tally Ho (since demolished) on the A1 and the Forester's Arms in Adwick, almost adjacent to the school field, and at the Aero transport café a mile up the A1 at the Red House service station. (KC)

Note: Mr Cockroft (personal communication, February 2005) asked me not to publish this section since "It will ruin my reputation"! Ron, nothing can taint your record.

The Happy Wanderer OR Ode to a Cross Country Run
We love to go a-wandering along the Roman Rig,
But when we do our feet appear so cumbersome and big.
And now down Red House Lane we go, the cemetery we pass,
It seems to be inviting us with branches and green grass.
And so we wend our weary way beside the old mill stream,
Until at last we reach the steps which are the test supreme.
We struggle on across the park and through the ruined fence,
And when we reach the changing rooms we cannot crawl from thence.
Oh may we go a-wandering until the day we die,
Killed by another run so dear in Mr Cockroft's eye.
                              Tony Waddoups L VI: School Magazine1953-54

Sports Day, Open Day & Cricket Week

The annual sports day was initiated in 1945. According to the School Magazine of December 1947: "On Wednesday, May 21st, we held our third annual Sports Day."

After the Easter holiday the school field acquired a totally new complexion with the marking out of the cricket field, the running track and athletics areas. Tennis nets and cricket training nets went up and the grass was regularly mowed. There was increasing activity and excitement outdoors as the summer term progressed - reaching, after the exams had all finished, a climax with Sports Day and Cricket Week. Football and hockey matches were played through winter and spring, but inter-house rivalry reached crescendo on **Sports Day.** With its vast array of track and athletic events, it came later to be held on the Thursday of the penultimate week of the summer term. This was usually the week containing St Swithin's Day (15th July) yet Mr Cockroft claims (Jan 2005) that "we never had a wet one"!

"**Open Day**" was held in the same week as Sports Day, when parents and other members of the community were invited to inspect the school's facilities and the activities and progress of the pupils.

The following week, normally the last week of term, was **Cricket Week**. In a sunny July, it was a most delightful time of the school year. *"That most valuable of institutions."* (SM 1958-59) For some, a time of romance but also of sad leave-taking. In this week the finals of the inter-house tennis were played off and from Monday to Wednesday there were three cricket matches against other schools, including the Doncaster School for the Deaf. Thursday was the day of the annual Staff vs School cricket match. Girls' PE teacher Miss Pat Lewin, in hockey shorts, would sometimes play for the Staff - a ploy calculated to unsettle the School wicket-keeper! (HS)

The Best Years? (last verse only)
And then towards the end of term,
The Cricket Week comes round.
A favourite with boys, I know,
That goes without a sound.
And all the boys and girls I know,

– At least in II AL –

Will say that school is not as bad

As many folk will tell.

Barry Daniels II AL. School Magazine 1954-55

Staff v School Annual Football Match (KC)

Cricket was always the gentleman's game and it was perhaps the more physical nature of soccer that got pupils – well, chiefly boys - salivating at the prospect of the annual Staff versus School football match. A real chance to see "Sir" feel some suffering! But it never turned out like that as both sides behaved better than certain spectators secretly hoped. The staff always acquitted themselves with honour, even though they probably lost more matches than they won over the years. They may have had the skills – but not quite the energy! In March 1951, for instance, School thrashed Staff by six goals to one.

For some years there was also an annual Staff vs School hockey match. In 1957 this was a close game where Mr McChrystal was credited with scoring a unique and winning goal, so "establishing the superiority of masculine brawn over feminine beauty." (SM 1956-57). In 1958 the match is reported in the School Magazine as "ending as a doubtful draw".

"It is only we who play badly who love the game itself." The Perfect Game: G K Chesterton, cited in the School Magazine 1949-50.

School Plays

In the early years there was a staff drama group and pupils fondly remember a production of "Charley's Aunt" in June 1947, which raised £38.3s.6d for school funds. The first school play involving some pupils was produced in 1943: "The Housemaster" by Ian Hay (BF). English teacher, Mr Greenwood (1947-52) is credited with establishing the school play "as a sound and flourishing dramatic tradition." (School Magazine 1952-53)

We owe tremendous gratitude to our teachers for organising and promoting the "School Play". A stage production was entirely beyond the horizon and the expectations of the average Percy pupil. It was a wonderful learning experience for those who ventured – or were pressed - to participate. Naturally, the English teachers took key parts as directors and producers. Mr Donald Rudd is remembered for some excellent productions in the fifties, particularly his "As You Like It" of December 1956. (SM 1956-57). Defending our rendition of Shakespearean verse in Richard III December 1954, Mr Rudd referred to the school being located "in a district whose inhabitants tend to have pronounced idiosyncracies of speech." (SM 1954-55). One supposes he meant our dialect, which was certainly not Shakespearean!

If you didn't aspire to being an actor there were opportunities in wardrobe, properties, scenery and lights (KC). The physics masters, Mr Powdrill and then Mr Dixon, were traditionally in charge of "lights" and German teacher Miss Crowe was an acknowledged specialist in the make-up department (DNP). Generations of "lights" volunteers recorded their names for posterity on the woodwork under the hall stage.

The December 1955 production of "Behind the Curtain" was reviewed as "very nearly good" and "Noel Pulman entered with ease into the lunatic fringe inhabited by Sir Rodney Redgood... ably supported by Diana Marriott. ... It was not a vintage year, but not a bad one either." (SM 1955/56).

As art master, over many years Mr Forrester was responsible for the sets, assisted in their construction by the woodwork and metalwork teachers. The quality of Mr Forrester's sets for "Charley's Aunt" was specially praised in the School Magazine of 1947.

A Midsummer Night's Dream – Revised Version for PJGS

"I had no judgement when to her I swore"	- Depressed culprit in school detention.
"I pray thee gentle mortal, sing again."	- Surely not a member of the Senior Choir!
"Oh, I am out of breath in this fond chase."	- Boy's lament on Cross Country Day.
"No doubt they rose up early to observe the rite of May."	- Early morning tennis fans?
"That is the true meaning of our end."	- Did GCE haunt Shakespeare too?
"Come recreant; come thou child: I'll whip thee with a rod."	- Things have not changed, obviously.

Unattributed: School Magazine 1957-58

School Choirs

There seems to have been a school choir, managed by the music teachers, from the time the school opened. Audrey Harrison (1942 joiner) recalls Miss Beati Havard-Jones running the choir with the assistance of history teacher, Miss Smith, who was an excellent pianist. Audrey also remembers a visiting teacher – "peripatetic", we would say today – coming to give violin lessons for a charge of threepence per week per pupil (AHR). In 1949-50 Latin teacher Mr McChrystal was teaching violin classes. (SM 1949-50)

A splinter group from the choir that had been temporarily augmented for the Christmas season busied itself in 1945 by carolling around selected houses in Woodlands, Skellow and Carcroft, collecting for charity.(RJ)

Mr Herbert Mayman joined the school as music master in September 1949 and remained until and beyond the conversion to comprehensive. His influence was recognised at the next Prize-Giving on the 11th November 1949: "The body of tone, delicacy of phrasing, and clear diction of the School Choir indicated a new high level of attainment." (SM 1949-50)

He became Senior Master from 1964. The greater part of the history of the school choirs – and of course the teaching of music - depended very much on him, on his enthusiasm and his professionalism. Many, many pupils acknowledge his influence on their interest in music. "An inspirational teacher" (CPE).

In September 1950 Mr Mayman founded a Senior Choir which was open to pupils and staff alike and very quickly acquired over fifty members(SM 1950-51). Whilst they rehearsed and performed separately, on appropriate occasions the junior and the senior choirs would perform together. As young people are reluctant to volunteer, Mr Mayman would personally select promising voices for the junior choir, but joining the senior choir – when voices had matured – was essentially voluntary (GBG), although he was known on occasion to canvass for more tenors and basses!

Many of us recall the voice test alongside Mr Mayman's piano, usually at the beginning of the new school year, when you would be required to sing a scale and be judged as to which range you belonged or, indeed, whether you were any good at all! (MS, CPE)

The choirs performed at school occasions such as Open Day, Prize-Giving and Christmas Carol service – Christmas Concert from 1956 - but also at wider events such as the annual Don Valley Choir Festival and the Barnsley Music Festival (CPE). The account of the 1952 prize-giving mentions "For sheer musical ability, phrasing and deftness of touch, the performance of 'Music When Soft Voices Die' by Charles Wood stood out among items which clearly gave as much pleasure to the performers as to the audience." (SM 1952/53).

The School Magazine records for May 1958 "…the choirs, whose faultless performance in the Music Festival at the Welfare Hall was a triumph. The senior choir especially has this year reached a standard of performance which it would be difficult to better." 1,600 pupils participated in this festival.

On several occasions the choir made records - vinyl LPs. About 1957 they recorded "Valiant for Truth", a motet by Vaughan Williams: *"After this it was noised abroad that Mr Valiant for Truth was taken with a summons, and had this for an answer…"* On the B side was a choral arrangement of the 23rd Psalm.

At the 1959 Don Valley Music Festival, the Senior Choir ambitiously presented a programme of Negro Spirituals which was very well received by the audience. (SM 1958-59)

Carol Service

The Carol Service was held each year at the end of the autumn term. As well as traditional English carols, a perennial feature, initiated by Miss Fell, was "Stille Nacht" (Silent Night) sung in German - in recognition of the fact that our first foreign language was German.

Dr "Butch" Tennenhaus taught a number of German songs to successive years and always rehearsed "Stille Nacht" before Christmas (GBG). For obvious reasons "O Tannenbaum" was sometimes rendered as "O Tennenhaus"! (RJ)

Dancing Lessons (KC)

Dancing lessons were run by the PE staff and were introduced at two levels:

* *Country and Traditional dancing* for the first, second and third

forms:e.g.Valeta, Barn dance, Military Two-Step, Gay Gordons, etc. It was most interesting to witness the changing attitudes of boys to the prospect of dancing lessons: from horror in the first year[*] to frisson in the third!

- *Ballroom or modern dancing* from the fourth form: e.g. waltz, quickstep, foxtrot, square tango. Apart from the PE teachers, maths teacher Mrs Pansy Land (née Crisp) was an enthusiastic teacher of ballroom dancing. Why was it that the girls were always much better dancers than the boys?

Derrick Moore (1939 entry) is credited with founding a school dance band in the 1940s with members from pupils and staff and with him as drummer. Physics master Mr Yarnold was the leader at one time. When modern Pop music was starting to establish itself, "Skiffle" became popular with teenagers and in the late 1950s John "Robbo" Robinson (1950 entry) headed a Skiffle Group which was a welcome "live" feature at school parties (BMcG).

Obviously, a big benefit of dancing lessons was being able to dance at the Christmas party, perennial highlight of the autumn term. Each formyear had its own party in the school hall in the last days of term - lower years in the afternoons and upper years in the evenings. This would include party games (according to age), dancing and possibly a small sketch or performance by volunteers on the stage. In requesting a dance, lessons were still being learned – for boys, braving rejection and for girls, bearing disappointment! Today it might be termed "confidence-building in a safe environment".

Air Training Corps (ATC)

In the latter years of World War II, the school's ATC Flight had camps at RAF

---

[*] Being macho miner's sons, as first and second formers we freaked at the prospect of dancing lessons. That was girls' stuff. However, since they were run in the gym at lunchtime, we would watch through the windows, and, thinking to make fun of the proceedings, would imitate the gyrations. We thus not only became familiar with the moves, but laid ourselves open to being led by the ear into the more formal instructional session. The shame of it! (RJ).

stations and even got airborne. Bill Bishop recalls flying as a teenager in the armed upper gun turret of a Lancaster bomber (though not operationally) and the temptation to pull the trigger to blast the Tiger Moth flying alongside! (WDB)

Raymond Hide served as sergeant in the school flight at one stage, recruited by its Officer Mr Fletcher, PE Teacher. (RH)

Field Trips (KC: **Prompted by a comment from Geoff Gravil**)

Apart from day excursions, senior pupils studying biology or geography would participate in residential courses. Malham Tarn Field Studies Centre was frequently chosen as it was well positioned for both subjects. By the 1960s archaeology was also being offered. Groups would take the train to Settle from where the Centre's Landrovers or mini-buses would ferry them six magical miles up through limestone country to Malham Tarn House, sitting in its lawns which sloped down to the lake. When one compares this setting with our pit villages it is easy to appreciate how Charles Kingsley, on a visit here from London a century before, was inspired to write "The Water Babies".

Specialised instruction by the Centre's staff was provided in classroom and laboratory, but the main emphasis was on fieldwork: identifying and recording features in the habitat. Being in the heart of the Pennines bad weather was often a risk, of course, but the schedule always had to be completed! The expedition in May 1955 experienced hail and snow. The arduous outings at the mercy of the elements promoted great camaraderie between participants, pupils and staff alike. The kitchen staff provided inter-esting sandwiches for our packed lunches, some based on peanut butter – which I had never tasted before.

At the end of the May 1951 biology field course, one Percy's student, having torn his only pair of long trousers, had to wear his shorts at the farewell dinner. He proposed a toast of "Here's Potamogeton in your Vasculum!" (SM) (Sorry folks, that's an exclusive for field botanists. KC)

An extra bonus of these courses was that they were shared by groups from several schools so we had the opportunity of meeting new people with shared interests.

This linocut appeared in many issues of the School Magazine

The School Badge

ADWICK-LE-STREET:

The Percy Jackson Grammar School.

Brief Description of Premises.

Site. Situated in the Parish of Adwick-le-Street, between Windmill Balk Lane and Tenter Balk Lane, adjoining the public park, and a short distance from the Great North Road.

Area. Twenty-one acres, of which the buildings and grounds occupy about three acres: the remainder gardens and playing fields.

Accommodation. The school, partly two storeys in height, accommodating 540 pupils, is constructed of steel framing carrying concrete floors and flat roofs, the outer walls being faced with Askern 2" light grey bricks. The exterior design is "modern" in treatment.

The rooms are as follows:—

Assembly Hall; Twelve classrooms; Library; Special rooms for Woodwork, Metalwork, Domestic Subjects, Art and Geography; Chemistry, Physics and Biology laboratories and a Lecture room; Medical Inspection and Rest room; Staff rooms and Secretary's room; Boys' and Girls' Prefects' rooms; Dining Hall and Kitchen with Store rooms; Cloakrooms, lavatories, etc. The Gymnasium and Changing rooms are connected by a covered way to the main block. There is a Caretaker's House near the main entrance gates.

Heating. A low pressure hot water system and automatically stoked coal-fired boilers have been installed. Hot water is supplied to all lavatory basins, sinks, showers and the kitchen from an independent boiler.

Lighting. Artificial lighting is by electricity.

Cost. The total cost of the site, buildings and equipment is approximately £62,000.

Plans. Prepared by the West Riding Education Architect, Mr. H. Wormald, A.R.I.B.A.

Furniture and Fittings. Supplied through the West Riding County Supplies Department.

COUNTY COUNCIL OF THE WEST RIDING OF YORKSHIRE

ADWICK - LE - STREET:

The Percy Jackson Grammar School

OFFICIAL OPENING

BY

SIR FRED CLARKE, M.A. (Oxon.), Litt. D.

(Professor of Education and Director of the Institute of Education, University of London)

ON

SATURDAY, OCTOBER 23rd, 1943

AT 2-30 P.M.

The programme for the official opening of the school on Saturday 23 October 1943

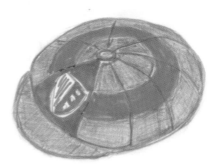

Boy's Cap 1940

Boy's cap 1950

School tie, blazer badge & Prefect's pin badge

Kathleen Gibson in full school uniform: 1940

School Magazine covers 1947-1968

Jeff Clarking's school magazine 1954-55:
As autograph collection (mostly staff; some pupils)

Prefects 1944

David Cranshaw, John Perrry, Derek Hutchinson, Cyril Knight, Jack Boyce, Bill Bishop
Joyce Reynolds, Gladys Hall, Unknown, Mary Hart, Eileen Hunt, Betty Oates, Joyce
McDonald, Iris Burton, Miss Banks, Mr Field, Mr Quine, Tom Cox

Cricket 1st Eleven 1944

D Whitnell Tom Howard David Cranshaw Stan McClusky Jack Butcher John Stocks
Unknown
Ray Bramham Tom Cox (capt) Mr Fletcher John Perry Bill Bishop

Football 1st Eleven 1944

John Perry , Stan McClusky , R Crosby , David Cranshaw , Bill Bishop,
Dick Whitehouse
Ray Bramham, Falconer? Tom Cox (capt), Jack Butcher, Jacky Firth

School Play 'The Admirable Crichton' March 1949

The Vicar	*Adjacent*	*Standing centre*	*On arm of armchair*	*Standing Right*
Mr Elliott	*Miss Crowe*	*Mr Fletcher*	*Mr Harrison*	*Miss Massey*

Teaching Staff 1945

John Good, Miss Hall, Miss B Mason, Dr M Tennenhaus, Miss Price, Mr Fletcher, Miss Smith, Miss Duke? Miss Havard-Jones, Mrs Outram (Secty), Miss Houghton, Miss Duke? Miss Hoyle
Mr Bell, Miss Anderson, Mr Harrison, Miss Banks, Mr Field, Mr V Milson, Miss Fell, Mr K Rocket, Miss O Gray, Mr W Quine

Percy Jackson Girls: Fruit picking 1944

Miss Hargreaves, Mary Hart, Unknown, Unknown, Eileen Hunt, Miss Banks, Gladys Hall, Margaret Hatfield, Iris Burton
Unknown, Unknown, Unknown, Audrey Kerry, Flo Brown, Barbara Mudd, Vera Ambrose, Margaret Padfield

A MERRY CHRISTMAS

AND

A HAPPY NEW YEAR

From

Jeff Clarking

Percy Jackson Grammar School

School Christmas Card from the 1950s

Class 2AL May 1952

Alan Brydon, Barry Paddock, Peter Graham, Clive Roberts, Roy Sylvester, John Crowther, Ken Cooke, Peter Rudd, Peter Oliver
Margaret Smith, Barbara Plumb, Pat Glover, Malcolm Palmer, John Robinson, Graham Hames, Norman Wainwright, John Atkins, Minnie Anderson, Sheila Wright
Dorothy Travis, Brenda Gillard, Vicki Jackson, Anne Limbert, Monica Beesely, Dr M Tennenhaus, Julia Phillips, Margaret Pidcock, Janet Lawton, Shirley Williams, Sylvia Hall

Percy Jackson Grammar School: Front Elevation 1955

Olympic Cyclist Roy Cromack.
July 1969:
490 miles so far today!

Teaching Staff 1955

Herbert Mayman, Unknown, John Jevans, Miss P Lewin, A McChrystal, Hazel Bilson, Eric Ormandy, Glyn Court, Miss Fish, W Ron F Cockcroft, W H Pilsworth

Miss Smith (Sectry), Miss G Bedford, Mrs L Richardson, Pam Land, David Haigh, George Horsfield, Alan Dixon, Joe Forrester, Tom Cox, Unknownm E L Hanson, Molly Marsden

Ken Muddiman, Kate Severn, Ralph Scurfield, Hilda Beal, W J Cunnington, Cecil Elliott, Miss Dent, Michael Tennenhaus, E M Mayers, Donald Rudd, Eileen M Crowe

Class 5AS 1955

*Barry Paddock   Roy Westgarth   Brian McGarrigle   Graham Hames   Harry Shaw
Barry Seymour   Brian Otley   Stanley Doyle   Albert Brydon   Peter Oliver
Jack Crowther   Roy Cromack   Peter Ward   David Thornhill   Les Holmes   Norman
Wainwright   Malcolm Palmer   Nigel Cottam   John Atkinson Robert Steadman
Margaret Smith   Dorothy Siddal Vicki Jackson   Christine Ashby   **Mr A Dixon** Sheila
Chester   Betty Smith   Anne Limbert   Sheila Wright   Margaret Pidcock*

Upper Sixth 1958

*Elaine Knowles   Keith Harrison   Joe Platts   Melvyn Key   Mick Lines   Derek Outram   Alan
Eborall   Keith McHugh   Brian McGarrigle   Alec Herring Mary Evans
Ann-Marie Burkett   Hilary Oliphant   Kate Short   Maureen Stevenson   Pat Witherington
Joyce Wood Hellen Trethewen   Paula Lawrence   Christine Moody   Jean Adams   Maureen
Temple
Clive Roberts   Barbara Hickling   Ken Cooke   Phoebe Hall   John Maxwell   Mr Cunnington
Mr Elliott Sheila Wright   Robert Saddington   Jean Marlow   Nigel Cottam   Kathleen Hall*

Teaching Staff 1966

Jim Smith, L Egarr, Ken Langley, Dave Robbie, S Sanderson, Keith Brooks, Mike Stables, Gordon Johnson, Jim Price, Sid Thrower, Derek Harrison, George Brooks, Jim Woodward, John Walton

Anne Rowland (Secty), Joyce Cole, Betty Rhodes, Unknown, Dorothy Horsfield (supply), Dennis Parrot, Mr Sandland, John Groom, Selwyn Rees, Unknown, Mrs Davies, Joyce Dixon, Rosemary Mead, Mrs Leek (Secty)

Ron Cockcroft, John Fay, Alan Dixon, Dr Alan Eslick, Eileen Crowe, John Mellhuish, Sheila Wood, Cecil Elliott, Herbert Mayman, Pam Land, Keith Muddiman, Molly Marsden, Derek Culley, Nancy Tag, John Hoyle

Brylcreem advert

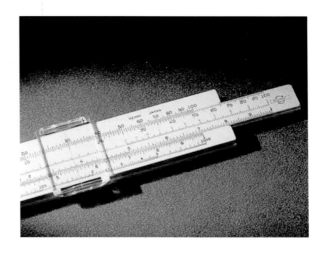

Slide rule

Bill Haley & The Comets

Buddy Holly & The Crickets

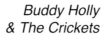

Marylin Monroe – The Seven Year Itch

Gone with the Wind

Snow White & the Seven Dwarfs

The Eagle

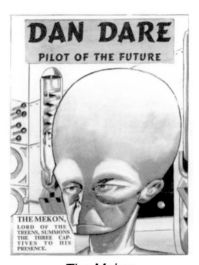

The Mekon

Tony Curtis

Jackson-Stein Reunion 3 – Loch Lomond June 2003
50 years after the original exchange 1953

Jackson-Stein Reunion 4 – On the Rhine – June 2004
50 years after the second exchange 1954

BBC Radio 4: Home Truths
Heinz & Ken with John Peel
Broadcast 9 October 2004

Fifty Years Reunion of 1956ers

Percy Jackson's Joiners of 1956 – Reunion on 28th September 2006

Back: Anthea Gillard, Gary Goodland, Ken Cooke (1950 joiner), Alan Avery, George France, Maurice Sanders, Alan Dixon (physics teacher), Alan May, David Kaye, David Etchell, Robert Mattock, Norman Bailey, Bernard Warner, Paul Bond, Stuart Knighton, Donald Rudd (English teacher), Howard Bugg, Barbara Fox, Joyce Brown, Heather Corney

Front: Pamela Pritchard, Joan Crane, Anthea Thornhill, Christine Fisher, Mrs Robert Mattock, Joan Turner, Marjorie Willoughby, Elaine Jones, Glenys Lawrence, Barbara Jones

Note: Teachers Ron Cockroft and Bob Oliver attended, but are not in the photograph.
Ernie Roberts (Head Boy 1946) and Margaret Pidcock (1950 joiner) also put in an appearance

The Percy Jackson Grammar School

1939 to 1968

"Keep Troth"

In this stimulating environment it was always possible that the occasional "holiday romance" developed, which would not necessarily be recounted to one's boyfriend or girlfriend back home! Visits to Malham were golden days.

School Scout Group, Beekeeper Club

At the request of a group of boys, the scout group was founded in 1940 by the head, Mr Field, but a year later it (in 1941) came under the leadership of English teacher, Mr Bill Quine. The first camp was held at Old Brodsworth in 1941 and in 1942 twenty school scouts camped at Brynbach, North Wales, where they could not have a fire at night due to black-out restrictions (SM 1947). In 1947 the group camped at Bilton, on the banks of the River Nidd near Harrogate, a site which was to be much revisited over the years partly, it was reported, because of the good treatment received from the local tradespeople.(SM 1949)

Locally, outdoor exercises were held frequently at Doncaster District Scouts' field site, "Squirrel Wood", near Burghwallis. In the early 40s the most exciting event of the school year was a dance organised by the scouts (DOM).

For most of its existence the scout group was ably led by woodwork teacher Mr Pilsworth (1946-1967). Could one say he specialised in both forms of woodcraft? (KC).

The **Beekeeper Club** started out as a section of the Science Club about 1951. It went from strength to strength and became a separate club under Mr Pilsworth's expert guidance and we usually had a hive or two in each quadrangle (DNP).

Mr Pilsworth retired in 1967, one of the longest serving teachers with 21 years service.

The Cosmopolitan Society

The CS was already active in 1947 and sponsoring delegates to conferences in London and Manchester. The society's aims were to learn about government and about life in other countries. The main programme consisted of talks by people, mainly guest speakers but also school staff and pupils, with personal knowledge and experience of certain aspects of work, life and problems in other countries. In the 1950s the *Daily Mail* used to sponsor Forums of Youth at regional locations.

At the Society's first meeting for the 1952-53 year, on 6th October, German teacher Dr Tennenhaus gave a very interesting account of his visit to Israel the previous summer. Inter-school meetings were held under the aegis of the Council for Education & World Citizenship (CEWC), enthusiastically promoted and supported by Miss Hilda Beal. In the autumn term of 1957 a group, augmented with members of the Geographical Society, attended the Girls' High School, Doncaster, to hear a lecture on "The Proposed European Common Market." In 1958 at Doncaster Boys' Grammar School, Iraqi student Mahomet Abdulla spoke on "Arab Nationalism".

Debating Society

Founded March 1952

     …. Modern Civilisation is a Failure. (defeated)

     …. The Emancipation of Women has gone too far.(defeated)

     …. The Sixth Form has too few Privileges. (result not reported)

The society seemed to fade quickly and was re-inaugurated in 1957…

     …. The Modern Girl is an Improvement on her Predecessors.(carried)

     …. Conscientious Objectors are justified in refusing to fight. (carried)

     …. Constitutional Monarchy is preferable in a Modern State. (carried)

(School Magazines)

The society metamorphosed in 1958 into the **Ormuzd Society**, open only to the sixth form and whose "primary aim is to provide a means by which the Form can widen its outlook on life" (Balkite 59/60). Ormuzd or Ormazd is the spirit of light and good in Zoroastrianism. As well as holding debates, the Society invited speakers and organised visits to a variety of cultural events, including music and theatre.

1958 topics:

     … There should be no law differentiating Sunday from any other day.

(carried 33 vs 9)

...Selective examinations should be abolished. (defeated)

In 1959 an interesting "double feature" was a visit to Sheffield to see a football match in the afternoon – Sheffield Wednesday vs Arsenal – and then on to an evening performance of Handel's "Messiah". Debating topics included:

Repeat – six years later
  ..... The emancipation of women has gone too far. (overwhelmingly defeated)
  .... The American influence on the British way of life is a menace. (defeated)
April 1959 .... Trade Unions should be abolished.

The Society was grateful for the support of several teachers including Mr Rudd, Miss Marsden and Mr Cunnington.

Other School Clubs/Societies

Chess	Mouse	Woodwork
Science (1950)	History	Geography
Theatre Group	Domestic Science	Gramophone Club
PT/Gymnastics	Boys Cookery (late 50s)	Girls' Woodwork (late 50s)
Photographic (1958)	Student Christian Movement	

School

It is five years,
Five fleeting years since I came here.
Five years of mixed emotions,
Laughter, tears, happiness and fears.
Five years spent with familiar faces –
O'Grady's grin, Huddleston's grimaces,
And all the girls with pretty - er... faces.
Latin scansion, the history note –
Learning of poetry by rote.
Crazy problems and lunatic sums,
Assinine questions that get my goat.
Why can't homework be put to the vote?
Don't think me a fool, or laugh, or jeer –
But despite the fact that School Cert looms near

Incredible fact! …. I like it here.

Harry Chambers VAL
School Magazine 1952–53

School Photographs

School photographs were not taken every year, but every second or third year so that a pupil would normally have had two class photographs if he left school at 16, and a third if he stayed into the sixth form. Photographs of the staff were taken at the same occasion which was normally near Easter. Organising the parade of each class before the camera was a task of military precision.

A report in the Magazine for the school year 1957–58 reflects: "Perhaps it is hoped that these records of our charm and beauty will inspire nostalgic memories when those portrayed are decrepit octagenarians*, but it seems odd to us that they never fail to capture the expression one would least wish preserved for posterity."

Early Days, by the Wag of '47
In its Entirety

Thought to have been written early in the year 47 AD!
School Magazine, Unattributed: Dec 1947, pages 34, 35.

> *Here beginneth the first chapter of the Epistle of St Percy, the son of Jack:*
>
> *At this time, in the country of the trees, near the city of the Donne, there exists a building overfilled with people of many clans.*
>
> *Yea, they are gathered together even from the clan of Bentley, and the clan of Skellow, and the clan of Askern.*
>
> *And here they are united in tribes, yea, verily the first tribe – this being the*

---

* **Well, some of us are there now! (KC)**
According to Brian Wallwork, when you reach 80 in Australia, you get the OBE : **O**ver **B**loody **E**ighty"!

last – and the second tribe, even up to the sixth tribe. But the first tribe has overflowed into the land of their neighbours.

And there are appointed elders in authority over them, each of his own religion, yea, even of the B1 sect and the D1 sect, and the sect of many tongues.

And the elders war with each other for the souls of the tribes, yea, especially for the second and third tribes.

And the tribes are united under four roofs, namely, Jack's House, the Washhouse, the Roadhouse and the House of the Blue Pencil.

And it is ordained that, at the first sounding of the timbrel all tribes and clans and sects shall congregate together that they may be presided over by the High Trinity, which doth govern all things, from the appointing of the elders, yea, until the sounding of the timbrel.

And at the second sounding of the timbrel, all clans and tribes shall disperse to the religion for which each is claimed, yea, verily to the B1 sect or the D1 sect, or the sect of many tongues.

And some shall sport and play and exercise themselves with stick and spheres and things: the night rakes combatting those from the laundry.

And a few shall practise the mystic arts of messing with pottage and spinning yarns. And others shall exercise their vocal chords, imitating the sweet music which heralded the arrival of Fritz and drowning the sound of the timbrel.

And the sounding of the timbrel shall announce the occasion of feasting, yea, of great jubilation, which shall be accompanied by shouting and appetising odours.

And an elder shall be there and a chief, and he shall bless the food and receive the tithes. And they shall feed on legumes and spheres of lepidoptera and unleavened bread.

Then they shall wander ad lib in the precincts among the trees till the time is passed, yea, till the sounding of the timbrel.

And each shall to his allotted task, till the final timbrel shall sound, yea, till the end of the day. Then shall each return to his clan, to the clan of Bentley and the clan of Skellow and the clan of Sprotborough.

And there shall be chariots there, and coaches, and they shall be called "Special" chariots.

And the elders shall travel in the first chariot – which is usually the last – and people of all tribes shall journey in the chariots, yea, even to Skellow and Askern and the City of the Donne.

Those only shall remain from the Blue Pencil House, and the House that Jack Built, who combat each other with spheres and sticks and things.

Woe be on the heads of those who incur the displeasure of the High Trinity and the Elders, for they shall remain in the building till the appointed hour.

Glossary & Notes – for the Uninitiated

Country of the Trees – Woodlands   **City of the Donne** – Doncaster

Clan – Village   **Tribe** – Form year

Sects – Specialities   **Chief** – Prefect

Elders - Teachers   **Religion** – Subject

Sect of many tongues – The languages stream.

Elders war with each other... Selection into specialities after first and second years.

High Trinity – The triumvirate of Headmaster, Senior Mistress and Senior Master.

The first tribe overflowed – Two first year classes were housed in Adwick Primary School.

Arrival of Fritz - Presumably German teacher Dr Tennenhaus, noted for his songs.

Occasion of feasting – School lunch.

Receive the tithes – Collect lunch tickets.

Spheres of Lepidoptera and unleavened bread – Moth balls (sago pudding) with shortbread bicuit.

Chariots – School buses

Remain...who combat each other - After-school inter-house matches.

Remain until the appointed hour... - Kept in detention.

CHAPTER 3

Memorable Events and Achievements

1939 Opening of the School

Whilst the school opened for instruction on the 9 October 1939, the official opening was not until four years later.

We are indebted to Norman Staveley of the Riley High School, Hull, for providing an original programme of the Official Opening. This commenced at 2:30 pm on Saturday 23 October 1943 in the school hall when Sir Fred Clarke, Professor of Education and Director of the Institute of Education, University of London, declared the school open.

1940s Homework Problem

Bill Bishop reports that in the 1940s electricity in a pit village like Skellow was supplied from the colliery's generator and whilst you were doing your homework the lights might go dim as a cage full of coal tubs was hauled up the shaft. (WDB)

Homework (3rd verse only)

And just before I go to sleep,

My thoughts towards tomorrow creep.

Then I sit up with a jerk,

I haven't done my maths homework!

Alan Ryans, 1C. School Magazine 1956-57

1940s Cloud-Spotting

There was one advantage in being in the geography A-level set, reports
Mollie Peet. Once a week before lessons began we got to go up on the
school roof with an RAF man who instructed us in the art of "cloud-
spotting", the forerunner of weather forecasting. Unfortunately he wasn't
the most glamorous of men – carefully chosen as such, I imagine, by
"Fanny" Banks (MPJ).

Early 1940s: First Full Set of Siblings are Pupils at PJGS

Len Park started at Percy's in 1941, joined in following years by his two
younger sisters, Rosemary and Ruth: the first full set of siblings to be pupils
at the school. Len left after School Certificate and enjoyed a career in the
seeds industry.

1944-1946 First University Entrants

The third form "founders" of 1939 reached the upper sixth for the 1943-44
year and Higher School Certificates were earned by four pupils: Tom Cox,
John Perry, Iris Burton and Joyce Reynolds. After completing military
service in the RAF, Tom Cox got a BSc at Leeds University in 1950. He
returned to Percy's as a maths teacher from 1952 to 1958. Joyce Reynolds
went on to work in broadcasting.

In 1945 Jack Boyce, who joined the second form in 1939, left for National
Service in the RAF. He later followed an illustrious career in the record
industry. Gladys Hall of that year obtained the National Certificate in
Teaching of the Deaf.

The founder first formers of 1939 produced in 1946 a bigger crop of under-
graduates: Don Bannister (English at Manchester, later psychology), Roy
Jackson (Chemical Engineering, University College London), Derrick
Hutchinson (Civil Engineering, University College London), William
Dennis "Bill" Bishop (Physics, Manchester), Stella (Mollie) Peet (English,

Durham), Mary Hart (Dom Science, Kings College London) and June Moore (Dom Sci, Kings College London).

Derrick Hutchinson's first professional job as a civil engineer was in the development of the site for the Festival of Britain (1951). He later worked for Costain on major construction projects, and spent many years in the Middle East.

Dennis Bishop developed and manufactured electrical components, including valves that were used in radios and TVs. He was involved in the production of 300 million glass-encapsulated switches for the first "electronic" telephone exchanges.

Don Bannister PhD (1928-1986) became a noted psychologist and a central figure in the development of Personal Construct Psychology (PCP) in the UK. He first worked as a Bevin Boy at Bullcroft colliery before taking up his university place. His experiences of life in a pit village and working down the mine are reflected in his novel "Sam Chard", published in 1979 (Routledge & Kegan Paul).

Roy "Jacko" Jackson PhD became a chemical engineer and spent most of his career with the Du Pont corporation in the USA.

Mollie Peet went on to graduate from Durham University. She married Dr David Jenkins, who became Anglican bishop of Durham.

Teacher Training: The 1946 leavers included about a dozen others who went into further education, mostly to teacher training colleges, and this was to be the pattern for many years. It was not until the 1960s that it became the practice for all aspiring teachers to take a university degree. Over the years the school produced a large number of teachers, many of whom were to become heads.

1939 Entrant: Key Figure in Classical Music Recordings

John "Jack" Boyce (1926-2004) joined the founding second form in 1939. He was a founder member of the Gramophone Club at school and became our second head boy. He left in 1945 for service in the RAF before taking a degree in botany at Liverpool University, but appears never to have worked in this field. His obituary in The Guardian of 2 October 2004 is headed: *"Imaginative executive responsible for a flowering of classical music recordings"*. It goes on to mention his "combination of Yorkshire outspokenness and wicked sense of humour".

Jack held important creative and executive positions in companies like EMI, Phonogram, Decca, Philips, Pye and Music for Pleasure. He was actively involved in two of the great recording projects of the mid-20th Century: the Decca Ring, conducted by Georg Solti, and the Philips Berlioz Cycle, conducted by Colin Davis.

He was co-founder in 1981 of ASV – Academy of Sound & Vision – which ushered in a rich diversity of recordings, including both period and light music, and – notably - the Lindsay Quartet with their famous sets of Haydn and Beethoven.

1945 Entrant: "The Quintessential British Bandsman"★
David Read FLCM FTCL LRAM ALCM
Son of a Welsh miner, David's family moved to Askern when he was just two months old. He was awarded an Industry Prize in his third year at PJGS. Already a talented cornet player with Askern Colliery Band, his reputation in the circuit grew rapidly and in 1953 he was recruited into the Regimental Band of the Welsh Guards. He returned to mining in 1956 but his real career was with the brass band movement. Through the 60s and 70s he won national championships as a soloist and as band member, later graduating into teaching, conducting and judging.

1947 Doncaster Floods
Based on an item in the School Magazine, Dec 1947.
At this time the River Don was tidal as far as the old mill weir at the bridge where the A1 Great North Road crossed it on the northern edge of Doncaster – near the Don Cinema. Just downstream, near Arksey and Kirk Sandal, the course of the river entered a serpentine which could substantially

---

★ Chris Helme at 4BarsRest.com, who also writes of David: "One of the brassband movement's most repected adjudicators."

impede the flow. This frequently resulted in flooding in the Bentley area. With the melting of exceptionally heavy late winter snowfalls in 1947 the river was in full spate and with the tidal flow pushing twice a day in the opposite direction it was inevitable that the Don breached its banks one Monday in March. This caused widespread flooding in Bentley and Arksey and also in Doncaster - around Dock Lane and the old fairground area.

The following day, to avoid flooding in Sheffield, lock gates on the navigable Don were opened there which resulted in a further surge reaching Doncaster. Even Toll Bar, north of Bentley, and two miles from the river was under water. It was over a week before water subsided from the residential areas – and much longer before the houses dried out. In later years the serpentine in the Don was straightened to some extent and the barriers were improved. These works were associated with the construction of the power station at Barnby Dun – which opened in 1960 and closed down in 1990.

1947 Start of a Distinguished Career

Professor Raymond Hide CBE, ScD, FRS.
In 1947 Raymond "Spike" Hide, the School's first State Scholar, entered Manchester University to read physics and then went on to get a PhD at Gonville and Caius College, Cambridge (SR), thus starting a distinguished research career in academic and government laboratories in the UK and USA, including several years as Professor of Geophysics and Physics at the Massachusetts Institute of Technology. A Fellow of the Royal Society (since 1971) and Member of the Pontifical Academy of Sciences (since 1996), he is now a semi-retired emeritus Professor of Physics at the University of Oxford.

1948 Entrant holds senior posts in the SSM

Charles Donald Wheat (joined 1948) took holy orders and followed his calling in the Society of the Sacred Mission, where he was known as Edmund. He ministered to a variety of communities and came to assume responsible positions in the SSM. He served two terms as English Provincial and for seven years was Director of the Society with responsibility for England and certain overseas countries. Much of his later career was spent in Northeast England where he continued working after his official retirement.

1948 School Visit to the London Olympics

Games teacher Mr Fletcher organised a day visit to the Olympics in London and invited Alan Dixon who at the time had been teaching at Woodlands Secondary Modern. Alan recalls "We had a great day out. The early train to King's Cross, breakfast at a Lyon's Corner House café and some wonderful athletics to watch."

1949 Major Intake of Staff

Eight new teachers joined in 1949, some of whom were to become "lifers": Miss Dent as Senior Mistress, Miss Burgess (German) and six male teachers: Ron Cockroft, Alan Dixon, Herbert Mayman, Ernest Powdrill, John Milburn and Arthur "Mac" McChrystal.

Ron, Herbert and Alan endured to the end of the grammar school days – a stretch of nineteen years - and stayed on with the Adwick School comprehensive.

1949–50 First Foreign Trips

Geography teacher, Miss Massey, arranged trips to Switzerland for parties of pupils (JH). In 1949, aided by Miss Wilson and Mr Horsfield, she led a party of thirty pupils for ten days in Switzerland. The wooden seats in the third class coaches of the train from Ostende to Basle left a lasting impression on pupils and the return trip from Basle to Doncaster took 34 hours, yet none of this diminished memories of the glorious Alps. (School Magazine 1948-49).

1951 School Excursion to the Festival of Britain

On 9 July 1951 a party of 300 pupils – about half the school! - and teachers travelled by train to the Festival of Britain on London's South Bank (SR). This mammoth undertaking would have required some six railway carriages and must have been the largest excursion ever undertaken by the school.

Margaret Skinner's (1950 joiner) overriding memory of this excursion was that she and a couple of colleagues were so fascinated with escalators - never seen before - that they rode up and down several times before they were ordered off by an attendant!

Percy Jackson Old Boy, Derrick Hutchinson, had worked on the construction of the Festival of Britain site in his first job as a civil engineer. (RJ)

1950/51 Intakes Produce Double Champions in British Cycling

In July 1969 two former pupils, Roy Cromack (1950 intake) and Christine Moody (1951 intake) respectively set new British national records for the men's and women's 24 hour race. Surely no other school can claim such a sporting achievement. Christine rode 427 miles and Roy did 507 miles, a record which stood for 25 years. In 1968 Roy was a member of the British cycling squad at the Mexico Olympic Games. (KC)

1950 Entrant – Brigadier in the British Army

Clive Roberts (1950-58) born in Highfields, known as an all-round sportsman at school, qualified BChD, LDS from Leeds University Dental School, and followed a career as a dental surgeon in the Royal Army Dental Corps. He was appointed honorary dental surgeon to HM Queen Elizabeth II in 1995 and retired as Director Army Dental Service in 1997 in the rank of Brigadier.

1951 Entrant Knighted – Sir John Rowling

John Rowling (1951-59), head of Nunthorpe School, Middlesborough, was knighted in the Queen's birthday honours of June 2003 "for services to education". (JH)

1952/53 First Oxbridge Entrants (SR/IMN)

In 1952 Joyce Hildreth got a place at Girton College, Cambridge.
The following year Deon Ward secured a place at St John's, Cambridge and Ann Gray became the school's first entrant to Oxford, Somerville College.

c 1952 Geoff Boycott bowled for a Duck

Physics master Alan Dixon reminds us that around 1952 the school cricket first eleven played the nearby Hemsworth Grammar School. There is a noteworthy entry on the scorecard : "Boycott G **0** : b Yeomans D". Our Doug Yeomans bowled for a duck the yet-to-be famous Geoff Boycott.

1953 Coronation of Queen Elizabeth II

In February 1952 Ken Cooke recalls "Jake" Jevans announcing at the beginning of a morning science class that King George VI had died. Mr Jevans had probably heard it on the radio in the staff room.

In the following year, on 2nd June 1953, many pupils watched the coronation of the new queen on black and white television, but for most of them it would have been on a neighbour's or relative's receiver as there were only about 40,000 TV sets in the whole country at that time – and the licence fee was £3. However, a coloured film of the pageant was rushed to cinemas around the country for the purpose of block viewings by schools and other groups. The greater part of the school attended the Gaumont cinema in Doncaster on 11 June 1953 to see "A Queen is Crowned".

The school collected donations towards the purchase of a "Coronation Bench" which was erected by the tennis courts and coronation mugs were distributed by school governor Mr J Wordley at the assembly before the Whitsuntide holiday. (School Magazine 1952-53)

1953 and 1954 – Anglo-German Exchanges (KC)
The Percy Jackson school exchanges were amongst the first to be made with Germany after World War II. We exchanged with the Freiherr vom Stein Gymnasium (boys) and the Neusprachliches Mädchen Gymnasium (girls) in Lünen, Westphalia. These two schools shared school buildings and attended in half-day shifts: boys in the mornings, girls in the afternoons and swapping shifts each week.

In 1953 sixteen girls and sixteen boys participated in the exchange and in 1954 28 girls and 21 boys. This led to a number of life-long friendships. Apart from attending school together, we made excursions and attended cultural performances. When our visitors came to England in 1954 we attended Shakespeare's "Coriolanus" at The Old Vic on the 3 April, where the stars were **Richard Burton** and **Claire Bloom**. On the 6 April we went to a performance of the Royal Ballet in Sheffield starring prima ballerina **Alicia Markova** (died Dec 2004).

Starting in 2000, a series of bilateral Anglo-German reunions of the exchanges – *Jackson-Stein Reunions* – began to be held: August **2000** Doncaster; June **2001** Lünen; June **2003** (50th Anniversary) Stirling,

Scotland; June **2004** Koblenz "Am Rhein"; June **2006** Llandudno.

Deutschland!   (Fifth verse only)

Ich fahre noch einmal dorthin;

Deutschland hat mich so bezäubert

O schönes Land, so lieb im Sinn,

Wie das Volk mein Herz geräubert.

Tony Waddoups UVI.School Magazine 1954-55

Germany!

I will journey once more to that magical land,

Of beauty and of love,

Whose people took my hand.

Translation. KC.

On the 9 October 2004 BBC Radio 4 "Home Truths" broadcast an interview recorded on the 15 September by John Peel (died 13 Oct 2004) with Ken Cooke and his German partner Heinz Wartenberg about their fifty year friendship and the history of the school exchanges.

1954 Entrant – Electronics Entrepreneur, Professor J David Rhodes

Prof J David Rhodes CBE FRS FREng DSc FIEE

Executive chairman (2004) of Filtronic Ltd, which he founded in 1977. He was a form prize winner in his first year at Percy's 1954-55 and went on to study electrical engineering at Leeds University. In 2004 he was awarded the Prince Philip Medal by the Royal Academy of Engineering for "outstanding contributions" in his field. The first recipient of this medal was Sir Frank Whittle, inventor of the jet engine (KC).

1955 Entrant – Globe-trotting TV Producer

Clem Vallance (1955-63) was key in producing in the 1990s a series of epic travel programmes for television, featuring Sheffield-born Michael Palin, e.g. "Pole to Pole"and "Full Circle".

1956 Entrant: Member of Senate of the Open University

David Etchell (1956-61) frankly admits to being a "slow starter" and left form 5G at PJGS without a glorious set of 'o'-levels. He went on however to take the professional exams of the Royal Institute of Chemisty and to become one of the first graduates of the Open University, of which he is a staunch and active supporter. As chairman of the OU Graduates Association he served on the Senate of the Open University. After a career of almost thirty years with the Scientific Service of the National Coal Board he took the PGCE teaching qualification.

For seventeen years he was a governor of Adwick School, the comprehensive school which succeeded PJGS.

1956 Entrant: HM Principal Inspector of Engineering In Mines

As could be expected of a school established "to educate the children of miners" many pupils from Percy's went on to work in the coal mining industry. The school yielded accountants, scientists, surveyors and mining, mechanical and electrical engineers, several of whom became pit managers or held other senior posts in the industry.

In this field, a leading example is **Gary Goodlad** Chartered Engineer, a fellow of both the Institution of Electrical Engineers and the Institution of Mining & Metallurgy. After working as an electrical engineer for the National Coal Board he joined the Mines Inspectorate of the Health & Safety Executive in 1974 as HM Electrical Inspector of Mines & Quarries and went on to become, in 1995, the Inspectorate's first HM Principal Inspector of Engineering in Mines. During his career he served on several national and international standards committees and on his retirement he received the British Standards Institution Certificate of Merit for 25 years service to standards writing.

"Permanent Feature" of Doncaster Market

Doncaster always had a thriving market, said to be the biggest in the UK. From the age of seven Bernard Warner (PJGS 1956-61) started helping out on his father's fishmonger's stall on "Donny" market. After leaving Percy's he spent a career of fifty years there and built the family business up to six stalls before passing it on to his nephew. In the 1970s Bernard was Branch President of the National Market Traders' Federation, representing

Doncaster's 600 stallholders with a multi-million pound turnover.

1957 – School Trips to Germany & Austria

The arrival (1956) of Mr George Brooks (German) and his wife Joyce (Geography) seemed to herald a new era in school travel. The School Magazine 1955-56 says that he was arranging for a group of three fourth form girls to exchange with their penfriends in Kulmbach, Bavaria, at the end of July 1957, whilst from the 10 August he was to lead a party of 18 third, fourth and fifth formers to visit the Austrian Tyrol, stopping briefly in Munich on the way home to link up with penfriends.

On the Munich trip John Bennett (1953 entry) was billetted with Klaus, who said his father was a plumber. He was – but he also employed about 600 men and their house had "more than one" bathroom! John enjoyed the luxury of an en suite bedroom.

1958 Governor J W Lane Retires

The Prize-Giving of 7 November 1957 was the last to be attended by Chairman of the Governors Alderman J W Lane. In his address he saw no reason "why the end of an innings should not be a happy occasion, particularly as he had 'carried his bat' in regard to the life of the school." (SM 1957-58) Indeed, in the early years of the school he was wont to say on his visits that "This school is my baby". (Joan Seymoor)

On 1 April 1958 Alderman J W Lane BEM JP "officially retired as chairman and member of the school's governing body, with a cheque of £42 presented from staff and pupils in recognition of his services both in getting the school built and in directing its affairs as Chairman of the Governors from 1939, the year of its opening." (SR). As a parting gift, Alderman Lane donated a cup for the purpose of an inter-house Spoken English competition. (SM 1958-59)

The Baby Boomers of the 1960s

Children born after World War II – from 1946 into the early 1950s - constituted the "Baby Boom" and these were the pupils who entered Percy's from 1957 onwards. Thus the last years of the school, from 1960 until 1968, belonged to the baby boomer generation.

Much has been written about the Baby Boomers and their reputation for being selfish and materialistic. 'Conspicuous consumption' was a phrase coined for this cohort. Yet they also produced the 1968 year of protest and a theme of idealism which ran through the following decades.

Thanks to rapidly improving economic conditions with corresponding advances in the media and technology, the last generation at Percy's enjoyed degrees of affluence and of influence hardly imagined by their predecessors of the 40s and 50s. Many of this generation are still economically active and are only now beginning to contemplate retirement.

c 1960 – Parent Teacher Association Formed

The prospect of Percy's "going comprehensive" aroused considerable consternation amongst staff, pupils and parents. A PTA was founded specifically to resist the change.

The battle was, however, clearly lost as reflected in the editorial to the shool magazine "The Balkite" for 1961-62: "On behalf of the whole school we feel it our duty to register a strong protest against our inclusion into the comprehensive system of education…." It went on to reflect very strong emotions about the change, repudiating claims of snobbery and class distinction, even stating at one point "All men are not equal and never will be: the differences between them are irreconcilable…"

Early 1960s – Explosion of School Travel

The late 1950s and early 1960s saw a massive increase in school trips in many forms. Significantly, the Youth Hostel Group was founded in 1958. The Scout Group had always held regular camps and some of the Societies made frequent forays, but in this era the expansion in travel was explosive. This was undoubtedly due to a combination of improved economic conditions and the import of younger teaching staff.

In the editorial of the first "Balkite" school magazine (1959-60), appreciation was given to all members of staff who had organised and assisted school visits, for it was recognised that "the area in which we live is notable neither for its cultural activity nor its natural beauty". School trips provided a welcome means of "escape from the industrial haze."

In the summer of 1961 there were tours both in the Black Forest and in Norway under the auspices of the School Youth Hostelling Group. In that year visits were also made to the Yorkshire Dales, Yorkshire coast, Lake District (in winter) and North Wales. For the year the Youth Hostelling Group recorded 160 pupils, on ten holidays, over 44 nights at 29 different hostels – an amazing total of 1,263 bed-nights! Credits are given to several staff members but particularly to Mr George Brooks, Mr Ron Cockroft and Mr Bob Oliver. (School Magazine 1960-61).

1960–61 The School's "Coming of Age"

On Speech Day, 10 November 1960, headmaster Chas Elliott sketched out the school's history from its "lowly beginnings in 1939" until its coming of age twenty one years later. (SM 1960-61)

The 21st anniversary was celebrated in some style at the end of that school year with a grand Garden Party held on the 15 July 1961. In contradiction of Cockroft's Law, this St Swithin's Day was however wet, but enjoyment was by no means dampened.

The school magazine, The Balkite, for 1961-62 records:

> "It is difficult to conceive a more varied programme of entertainments and activities than was offered to the public. They could buy almost anything, they could see a first class show, send balloons to distant places, bowl at skittles, ride a chairlift, dip in a bran-tub, smash crockery, even purchase 6d worth of horror in a "Tunnel of Terror". And all these things they did with enthusiasm and open-handedness.
>
> Lady Jackson herself, having opened the party, indulged in almost all the activities, as did the headmaster.
>
> So reckless was the spending, so enthusiastic and persuasive the helpers that, at the end of the day, with all bills paid and all claims met, the profit was found to be over £350. To select any individual for special praise would be invidious, but if one group were to be lime-lighted it must be the Domestic Science Section, without whose efforts the profit would certainly not have topped £300."

Physics master, Alan Dixon, explains that the "Tunnel of Terror" was created in the air-raid shelters with lighting and sound effects provided by the physics department. The copious buntings decorating the school that day were provided by the Hull Trawlers Association whilst Brodsworth Miners' Welfare loaned fairground equipment. Owing to the wet weather, the rifle range was moved indoors to the physics laboratory, which resulted in many rifle pellets being embedded in the back wall of the lab. These were subtly covered by a poster until redecoration about three years later.

1962 Inter-House Music Competition

This was inaugurated in the summer term of 1962 and included solo performances and house choirs. The trophy was presented by Miss Bintcliffe.

1962 Record Number of Oxbridge Entrants

Four boys were accepted for Cambridge University in 1962: Peter Davis, David Buxton, Andrew Brunt and Clem Vallance.

1962 New Subjects

Economics and Russian were introduced as new subjects at sixth-form level. The number of sixth-form students reached 123 – the first time it went over the hundred mark (SR/IMN). From the early 1950s the emergence of the Soviet Union as a world power was becoming recognised and hence the relevance of Russian language as a useful school subject.

1962 Latin Scholar becomes Director of EMI Records UK

Keith Staton was at Percy's from 1962 to 1969. After leaving university with a degree in Latin, he taught for a short spell but then joined the sales department of EMI Records UK, eventually becoming Sales Director and leaving in 1993. He now operates his own music distribution company.

1966 Economics Teacher "Fraud"

Head, Chas Elliott, records on 29 March 1966 "Mr Jones, economics master, reported he had misappropriated Italy tour funds – over £2,000 !" (SR)

1966 Long-serving Caretaker Dies

Mr Butcher, caretaker for over twenty years, died in April 1966 after an emergency operation. Reported in the school records as "A good and faithful servant".

1967 Kitchen Supervisor Resigns

The school roll reaches 890, with 130 in the Sixth Form. A three sitting system is introduced for school lunches, which Miss Brown, Kitchen Supervisor, finds too much and resigns on 28 September. (SR/IMN)

Pupils of the New School Fly High in Pharmaceuticals

David Winwood and Paul Edwards were accepted into PJGS but by the time they joined in September 1968 it had become the Adwick School. They thus received their secondary education entirely within the newly founded comprehensive and were classmates thoughout.

David Winwood went on to take a PhD in chemistry and following a research career in medicinal chemistry, became Associate Vice Chancellor of North Carolina State University, one of the leading universities in science and technology in the USA.

Paul Edwards graduated in chemistry and followed a successful career in the pharmaceuticals industry with companies such as Beecham, Genzyme and Genemedix. He later specialised in senior and board level search. In 1997 Paul was awarded the MBE for services to biotechnology.

1968 Percy Jackson's Ceases to Exist

During 1967-68, to ease the transition from grammar school to comprehensive both for pupils and for staff, the fourth form and first year sixth were taught jointly with the relevant age group from Adwick High School, although the two schools remained independent with two heads! (FJA)

Writing in the "Balkite" in 1968, the final magazine of the grammar school, head Mr John Atherfold said:

> "The new school which will emerge will have certain traditions and qualities as part of its birthright, handed down from Percy Jackson Grammar School and Adwick High School, and the task before the staff and pupils is to harness the

best from both schools and use them as the springboard to future development and success.

"The future of this school presents an exciting challenge to all concerned. Fundamentally, however, what matters most is the work, effect, achievement, attitudes and aspirations of the pupils themselves. I have every confidence that they will rise to meet the challenge."

Classes at the Percy Jackson Grammar School ended with the close of the summer term on 31 July 1968 and the official close of the school was 11 August. From the 12 August (the "Glorious Twelfth"!) the premises became home to a new comprehensive school called Adwick School (FJA). In 2006 the school is known as North Doncaster Technology College with some 1600 pupils and over a hundred staff.

CHAPTER 4

Cultural Background to the 40s, 50s and 60s

A socio-philosophical contribution by **Brian "Mac" McGarrigle**

Those were the Days!

If you were a teenager in the 1950s, when Dennis Compton played a straight wicket and kept a straight parting with the aid of Brylcreem, then you will read this *History* with automatic understanding of the culture which lay behind all that happened. However, if you are a child of more modern times, you may wonder at some of the things described here. It may help therefore to give a description of the thinking and tastes of the 40s, 50s and 60s. I do not attempt to be unbiased in my comparisons. No-one is unbiased. My biases will be self evident. I am a child of my times.

A quick and striking way to define those times to someone who is young today is to declare many of the things which we did not have:

Personal computers; jeans; anoraks; punk music or fashions; rap music; homosexuals, bisexuals, trisexuals, transsexuals, transvestites, homophobia;

homophilia; drugs, chauvinism, political correctness, Common Market - EU, video games, CD's, body art; liberated women; women prime ministers; New Labour; paparazzi; Lady Di; degenerate Hollywood movies; Costa Lotta; Florida; teacher abuse; slaughter of schoolchildren; motorways; KFC; McDonalds; supermarkets; TV dinners; filter tips; latch key kids; persecution of friendly rural fox hunters; comprehensives; anti-smoking campaigns; Muslims; IRA;

By now some of you are thinking "This is nonsense. Lots of those things existed then." So I have to admit, well, yes, they did - sort of. By this I mean they did exist but not as we know them today. They either were not a problem, or not talked about, or taboo, or not thought about and so were a negligible part of the social fabric and might as well not have existed as far as the average child of our times was concerned.

So we did not have much of the drama of modern times. Despite a recent war, these were relatively peaceful and more gentle times. Some of the things we did have (in contradistinction to the above) were:

Slide rules (whoa! what's that?); log tables (eh?); suits, sports jackets and flannels; Teddy Boys; Spivs;Tony Curtis or James Dean hairstyles; rock n roll (early); heterosexuality; marriage; fags (English slang not U.S.); real ale; gentlemen, ladies; Wirtschaftswunder; Froggies; Eyetyes; playing cards; LP's, EP's and 78 rpm records; nail polish; femininity; middle-aged male prime ministers mostly psychologically defeated by the experience of two world wars; Old Tired Labour; Our Parliamentary Correspondent; Diana Dors; wholesome Hollywood movies; Skeggy; London; corporal punishment; well behaved children; A1 - Great North Road; Wimpeys; Grocers; Butchers; shops; fish 'n chips for 11d; Woodbines; going home to a house with a mother in it; fox hunting; grammar schools and secondary moderns; pro-smoking campaigns; Christianity; leprechauns.

Again some of you are thinking (and it's the same ones, I see) "This is nonsense. Many of these things exist today." Again I have to admit that they do but they are not the same. They don't dominate as they used to. A society is defined partly by what it has and does but also by its priorities and many of these have been turned upside down. In the 40s, 50s and 60s buggery was a crime and a cause for social ostracism, yet smoking was a commonplace social activity (q.v. Princess Margaret). Now buggery is legal and ever so trendy while smoking is about to become a crime and a cause for social ostracism. This is change, but is it progress?

Children's behaviour

Children were better behaved. Why? Because the crimes or bad things to do had simply not occurred to them. Step one, in any misdeed, is that it has to occur to you. The idea has to enter your mind. If an idea is unknowable or unthinkable then it is undoable. It's that simple. In the last third of the 20th century, the papers, TV and most blatantly, Hollywood movies, have joined a race to the bottom where each outdoes the other in pandering to the basest instincts of human nature.

There is a grossness and amorality in today's culture and in the news and entertainment media which is beyond shocking to the mind of a person who grew up in the second third of the 20th century and has the good sense to think for him/herself. Today's children have been raised in a culture in which no crime or misdeed is unknowable or unthinkable. So the first step in any crime has been provided for all children. It just remains for some of them to take the second step. In the second third of the 20th century parents and teachers simply did not tolerate disrespect. You had to respect your elders and superiors and civilization flowed from that. There was corporal punishment, although opposition to it was growing, but there was also a consensus that a certain "order" was natural and essential.

Courting

In conversation with a girl, a boy would be very careful about what he said. He would not swear and would never expect to hear a girl swear. There would be very little discussion of things sexual. Any such discussion would be inoffensive. Girls were assumed to be virgins unless they gave some strong indication to the contrary. Boys were probably 90% virgins also. The difference was that boys would not admit to being virgins, while girls would not admit to not being virgins. Every boy wanted a virgin for his wife but not necessarily for his girlfriend. Girls were aware of boys' thinking on this matter – but were not entirely in sympathy with it. For them it was a Catch 22. They had to figure out how to become a wife without becoming a girlfriend.

What could a boy and girl do then? Well you could meet in the school lunch break, exchange a few words between lessons, go for a walk, play tennis, sit on the grass and flirt. In the evenings you might go to your local youth club, progressing later to going to the pictures, dancing at Berry's, The New Baths or the Doncaster Co-op ballroom, going to a pub or jazz club with Trad jazz, going for dinner (bit expensive). One studiously shunned Ilkley Moor or any girl called Mary Jane. Forewarned is fore-armed!

The introduction of jukeboxes, giving access to current pop music, into cafés such as Priestnall's provided a new diversion for teenagers in the 50s (DNP). A casual or more formal appointment could be made to meet in one of the "coffee bars" as they started to be called. Two challenges there became: how long dare one respectably linger over one cup of coffee – and who will be next to put another sixpence in the jukebox? There were no phones in homes so you always had to make a new date at the end of each date or else you were in limbo. Also nobody had cars, so you met downtown under the clock or outside the cinema. The boy would walk the girl back to her bus or, if the last bus had gone, walk her home and then walk back home himself! But of course, if she gave him a kiss (or two) he was walking on air!

Romance

.... Come to the pictures, he said. That was the beginning of an idyllic summer. They had played tennis, they went for long walks, they had cultural evenings with records and ten cigarettes. They even, though it wasn't really their line, slummed it at the Co-op dancehall. They waited for the exam results and despaired of having achieved "the required standard". He called her his flower of the pit tips – rose of the slag heaps. They were in love..........

.... The summer drew on to September and the sweet afternoons were filled with desperation as she was going to university and he was staying on to try for Oxbridge. - These autumn afternoons are so unexpected, he said one day. Keats was quite right...Why are you crying? – I don't want it to end. – There'll be plenty more autumns. – But not like these.

The first letter she had at university began: At this very moment you are getting into the train which will take you away from me.... How can I exist till you return?

But he was still alive six weeks later when she told him
she'd never loved him anyhow… not really.

Extracts from "Romance" by **M Witherington, The Balkite 1968**.
See also Chapter 2, "Cricket Week".

Dancing

Here perhaps is the litmus paper of any society and the biggest contrast between then and today. The main difference is that we used to dance and today people simply don't. They wriggle and gyrate and contort or sway arthritically without a dance step to their name. Once upon a time a boy needed a girl to dance with and vice versa. If two girls attempted to do anything so shocking as dancing together (except in dance practice) they would soon be told to stop.

There was also no "moon dancing" i.e. holding the girl close to slow music and forgetting to move your feet. The reason boys and girls needed each other was that they knew dances with dance steps. The boy and girl had different but synchronized and complementary steps to do in unison. There was the waltz, quickstep and foxtrot (bit tricky). There was also jive or bop when rock 'n roll music came along. Finally there were Latin American dances – tango, cha cha, samba (very, very tricky) for the ultra suave aficionados. The latter were always married men with wavy hair and moustaches and pound notes and cigarette lighters and cars that went vroom-vroom. They always stole away your nice virgin girlfriend and you vowed to get married someday, grow a moustache, have your hair waved and learn the cha cha.

> Cars that go vroom in the night
> Should really not give you a fright
> It's the girl in the seat
> Who'll be feeling the heat
> Unless she puts up a good fight.

(Apologies to Spike Milligan)

Popular Music

Music, as someone once said, is the sine qua non of la dolce vita (was it John

Preston?). Music comes in two kinds. Good music and bad music. It's very simple really. The difficulty arises when people try to classify which is which.

In the 40s big swing bands dominated and singers were merely accessories to the bands, although in the war years Vera Lynn made great hits as a solo singer. Bing Crosby and Frank Sinatra branched out successfully as singers in their own right and after World War II the bands faded till by 1950 no band could make it into the Top 20.

For the first half of the 50s crooners dominated and foremost was Frankie Laine who belted out ballads as never before. The turning point from ballads to rock n roll was Bill Haley's "Shake, Rattle and Roll", the first rock 'n roll million seller (before Elvis whatsisname). Riding Haley's coat tails was Elvis with "Heartbreak Hotel" which gave rock 'n roll a new direction with sex appeal and raunchiness. In the late 50s Elvis went into the army and became feeble. After coming out of the army in 1960 he went into movies to make the worst films of all time and the worst music of all time. Never has a talent been so debased.

Notable in the UK in the late 50's was Lonnie Donegan who started the skiffle craze and got a US number one with "Rock Island Line". Lonnie had a personal affinity with Doncaster's Gaumont theatre and kept a house in Bentley. His No 1 Hit "My Old Man's a Dustman" was recorded live at the Gaumont in February 1960 (Yorkshire Post). Incidentally – it was skiffle that got the Beatles started.

Round about 1963 the Beatles began to be big - thanks to cognoscenti like me who bought their first single! The sound was catchy and they were on UK TV and they were "ours". Their sound didn't become unique till records like Eleanor Rigby when they and George Martin invented orchestral (unbounded) rock. The Rolling Stones were anti-Beatles, counterculture, ugly boys and specialized in raunchy songs and getting thrown out of London restaurants for not wearing a tie. The late 60's saw an explosion of rock talent whose recordings dominate radio even now, due to the paucity of talent since. Some of the defining talents and songs of these decades were:

1940's

We'll meet again - Vera Lynn; Mares Eat Oats [Mairzy Doates] - The Merry Macs; Ghost Riders in the Sky - Vaughan Monroe; White Christmas - Bing Crosby; I'll Never Smile Again - Frank Sinatra; You'll Never Know - Dick Haymes; Paper Doll - Mills Bros. In the Mood - Glen Miller;

1950's

Nola - Les Paul; Jezebel - Frankie Laine; Harry Lime Theme - Anton Karas; Unforgettable - Nat Cole; Cry - Johnnie Ray; Secret Love - Doris Day; Rock Around the Clock - Bill Haley; Heartbreak Hotel - Elvis; Rock Island Line - Lonnie Donegan; Love and Marriage - Frank Sinatra; Peggy Sue – Buddy Holly; Honky Tonk - Bill Doggett. Move It -   Cliff Richard;

1960's

Apache - The Shadows; Please, please me - Beatles; Eleanor Rigby - Beatles; I Want to be Your Man - Rolling Stones; White Room - Cream; Strangers in the Night - Frank Sinatra; Good Vibrations - Beach Boys;

It is most striking to note how much music changed over those 30 years and to wonder why. Is it a reflection of the kind of people in our society, the progress of democracy or the advances in technology? In the 40s music was very melodic and lyrics were poetry of the best kind (Cole Porter etc.). Sentiments were of love and romance and optimism. There was absolutely no evil as there is today (Eminem and the like). Perhaps this was because, in wartime, people wanted love not war and perhaps because society was more civilized.

Then came rock 'n roll with the wild beats and (to adults) incomprehensible lyrics which often didn't matter a damn anyway. Today we have rap which has to be the most degenerate musical art form ever and which is based on hate. How did our civilisation get to this? There is also a revival of swing and crooning ballads (Celine Dion) so perhaps there is a glimmer of hope for some of today's youth. Thank goodness for Cliff who bestrides the decades like a colossus with hit after hit – and of course Mick and Paul.

Pestering Pops

Today pop groups are all the rage. We are pestered by the Beatles, followed by the Shadows, outpaced by the Pacemakers, pricked by the Hollies, outslept by the Dreamers, beaten by the Gamblers, crushed by the Rolling Stones and now we are chasing the Breakaways, blown over by the Tornadoes and washed away by the Merseybeats. So be careful – don't buy the Searchers!

D J Rush 5GA, The Balkite 1963-64.

Clothes

Clothes used to matter. The main difference between today's society and the 40s/50s generations is jeans. Today jeans have proliferated like a plague to become a fashion cop-out for all and sundry. In the 40s and 50s boys and girls dressed like boys and girls respectively. Boys wore short trousers to about 14 before graduating to long trousers - which was a very big deal.

Girls did not wear trousers. An adult male, fully kitted out, wore a two- or three-piece suit, a shirt and tie, possibly a pullover (somewhat gauche), overcoat, scarf, gloves and – maybe - a trilby hat. Ladies similarly had many layers of clothing (central heating was in its infancy.) Skirts and dresses were long and voluminous. There was no such thing as panty hose. Only silk or nylon seamed stockings. Ladies were happy to be feminine and most of all to look respectable. They did not want to appear "common", though that might have been a subjective standard.

The middle 50s were remarkable for the Teddy Boy Suit with drainpipe trousers with turn ups, very long jacket, square cut front, one link button, Slim Jim ties (all available from the Danum Clothing Co.), crêpe-soled shoes and Tony Curtis hair style This was started by the toffs in Saville Row and spread down to the proletariat. It could be done moderately and tastefully or taken to ludicrous garish extremes by yobbos. In about 1957, when we were in the sixth form, Robbo started a trend for us when he turned up one Saturday night in a suave charcoal grey made-to-measure suit and this became de rigueur for our set. For £20 we got a made-to-measure two- or three-piece suit and were as suave as hell. And the Teddy Boy suit was a goner.

Films

The cinema was a magical place where you escaped from pedestrian everyday life and were spirited away to distant lands and thrills and laughs for two or three hours. It used to be that you got to see two films and the news. They showed non-stop from noon till 11 p.m. so, as kids, you could watch the big picture twice and you could go in at anytime and just keep watching till you realised "this is where I came in". At local cinemas mothers sometimes had to come and find their children, the usherette shining her torch along rows of little faces in the cheap seats until the mother cried "There he is!"

Films were rated U for universal and A for adult where you had to be 15 to get in. But everything was very tame by today's non-standards. A horrific event was portrayed by showing the face of an actor filled with horror - they did not shove blood and guts in your face as they do today.

> **Comedy stars** were Laurel and Hardy, the Bowery Boys, Abbot and Costello, Danny Kaye, Dean Martin and Jerry Lewis (US), Frank Randle, Old Mother Riley and Kitty, George Formby, (Big hearted) Arthur Askey, Norman Wisdom, Alastair Sim and George Cole (Belles of St. Trinians), Peter Sellers (UK).

> **Dramatic/Romantic stars** were Dirk Bogarde, Jack Hawkins, Trevor Howard, Larry Olivier, Laurence Harvey, Kenneth More, James Mason.

> **Sex symbols** were Diana Dors, Janette Scott, Muriel Pavlow, Margaret Lockwood, Deborah Kerr, Joan Collins (still knocking them dead) , Glynnis Johns, Liz Frazer (UK), Marilyn Monroe, Patricia Medina, Ingrid Bergman, Mamie Van Doren, Jayne Mansfield (US).

Films were mostly comedies, adventure, romance or drama. In addition there was a huge number of British war or wartime movies which were always jolly well done: The Colditz Story, The Cruel Sea, Dunkirk, Rommel etc. The cast always came from the same twenty British actors, and it was always the same ones who were officers, putting on a jolly good show with lots of stiff upper lip, and the same ones who were privates taking bleeding liberties and ne'er the twain shall meet, except for John Mills who got to be an officer and a private! The other type of picture was a wild west cowboy featuring Roy Rogers etc. These could be excruciatingly boring even to a child.

But boring movies can serve a purpose. We had a practice of going to the Don Cinema on a Sunday night when they would show some really corny old film. Since the dialogue was borderline imbecilic we would heckle the actors all the way through with extremely witty remarks - which only a grammar school education and intellect could come up with! This made the audience laugh and the management didn't seem to mind at all - an excellent example of British humour and improvisation and making the best out of a bad job.

The best way to compare films of today and films of then (40s,50s,60s) is to look at the top ten movies of all time. This list was made by the British Film Institute and is based on the number of admissions (not box office receipts.) When you consider that the price of admission was 10d (= 4p) in 1948 and £5 today, it is nonsense to talk about "Titanic" being the most popular film of all time. So, based on admissions in the UK we have:-

The Ultimate Film: Nos. 1 to 10.

				Admissions (million)
1	GONE WITH THE WIND	Clark Gable	(1940)	35
2	THE SOUND OF MUSIC	Julie Andrews	(1965)	30
3	SNOW WHITE & THE SEVEN DWARFS	Disney	(1938)	28
4	STAR WARS	R2D2	(1978)	20.76
5	SPRING IN PARK LANE	Anna Neagle	(1948)	20.5
6	THE BEST YEARS OF OUR LIVES	Frederic March	(1947)	20.4
7	THE JUNGLE BOOK	Disney	(1968)	19.8
8	TITANIC	Leonardo DiCaprio	(1998)	18.91
9	THE WICKED LADY	Margaret Lockwood	(1946)	18.4
10	THE SEVENTH VEIL	James Mason	(1945)	17.9

Only two of these were made later than the sixties. Of the non-cartoons, all but one featured British stars.

I think films of the 40s, 50s and 60s are best contrasted with the films of the 70s, 80s and 90s by saying that as a child, when coming out of a movie my spirits were lifted and I felt elevated while in the 80s my spirits were depressed and I felt degraded from the experience and hence stopped going. Thank heavens for videos and old movies: Glynnis is always there for me. I'm coming Glynnis!

Comics

Before TV, children loved British weekly comics which could be ordered and delivered with the morning paper on most weekdays. Beano (Big Eggo) and Wizard on Tuesdays; Knockout and Comet on Wednesdays ; Thursdays Dandy, Rover and Hotspur; and Fridays Eagle (Dan Dare vs. the Mekon) and Champion. They were mostly drawn pictorial comics (2d) but Wizard, Hotspur, Rover and Champion were strictly text serial stories of adventure (3d). So there was serious reading involved – nothing as passive as watching TV. There was quite a trade between lads "swapping comics" and in Doncaster there were a couple of shops where you could buy and sell used comics (DNP).

An example of a story was one in about 1947 about Big Nosey who was cursed by a witch so that his nose grew to be about 3 feet long. He had to find herbs and potions of exotic ingredients (eagle's egg, bat's dandruff) to put on his nose to shrink it. Each week he had an adventure and found an ingredient and shrank his nose a few inches. This was obviously a spellbinder and, as you trudged home after school in the cold and the wind and the rain of a dirty winter's night, it was only the thought of sitting by a nice big coal fire in the lamplight and finding out what was going to happen to Big Nosey which kept you going!

However such luxuries as comics did not come until after the war. If you were 4 in 1943 and went to the newsagent to order the Dandy (Korky the Cat, Desperate Dan) you were told that there could be no new orders until after the War! When was that going to be?.... The whole duration of the War with no comics! Now you've heard everything about the horrors of the War – and we survived this!

King Coal

Coal fires were the most magical thing in the childhood of any kid in the '40s.

> They could roar. They could crackle. They could spark.
> They could flicker and glow and light up the dark.

You could see faces in the gentle inferno and towers and mountains and birds and animals, limited only by your perceptiveness and imagination. Fires preserved the life of every soul in the United Kingdom and protected them from the icy draughts which were a design feature of all British houses of that time. For hundreds of years British architects had been secretly instructed by the government to ensure that a number of subtle draughts were built into all houses. This was a precaution against invasion. If ever Britain were conquered, we knew that the invaders could never survive in our homes and buildings. Only a Briton born and bred could survive those draughts. (The same principle as H.G. Wells War of the Worlds where the Martians can't survive Earth's bacteria).

You could never get rid of all draughts. You could lay rugs at the bottom of all doors and great heavy curtains over all windows but still there was a draught coming from somewhere. You could feel it on the right side of the back of your neck or sometimes your left kidney. You could use a candle or a match or a cigarette to detect most of them but there was always a mysterious draught which you could feel but not find the source of. So you poked the fire and huddled closer. When coal fires began to fall into disfavour you knew that the British Empire was coming to an end due to cultural mutilation. No empire can survive when it snuffs out the source of its life.

Coal was black shiny hard stuff. Like low grade black diamonds. You burned it in a fireplace with a cast iron grate and a brick chimney. Lighting the fire required great skill:

1. Screw sheets of newspaper into tight – but not too tight - balls and lay in the grate.
2. Lay firewood kindling on top of papers.
3. Lay smallish pieces of coal on top of fire wood (No large pieces dummy. They'd never light)
4. Light paper at front bottom and at back.
5. Watch carefully as the fire spreads through the layers and the coal crackles and sparks and catches fire.
6. If it's slow going, place a large newspaper (The Times or Y.E.P) over fireplace with a gap at the bottom and watch it roar in the draft.
7. Watch for brown patches appearing in the newspaper and immediately whip it away and crush it into a ball.
8. Enjoy.
9. Top up the coal from time to time.
10. Poke it from time to time to make sure all the coal gets burned.

Really good coal would have lighted gas jets purring out from it. British homes always had an armchair on either side of the fireplace and a sofa in front. Coal was kept in a scuttle by the fireplace. If you were a kid you could lie in front of the fire and toast your back. "Get away from that fire! You'll give yourself varicose veins! You'll be sorry! I'm not going to tell you again! If your dad comes in, and sees you lying there, you know what's going to happen!!" You could sit all night talking by the fire watching it glow and burn - cosiness upon cosiness. And when finally the fire went out you knew you had to retreat to bed before the drafts got you.

You could dispose of a lot of rubbish on the fire. Fag packets. Bills. Potato peelings. You lay the peelings on the back of the fire and they would sizzle nicely and pop and give a wonderful aroma of damp socks.

Mining families were entitled to a generous ration of coal, about a ton per month, but they had to go to the pit yard office to order the next delivery and pay a nominal handling charge. Traditionally the coal lorry would simply tip your load at your front gate and it was left to the family to move it to their bunker, coal-house or "*coal 'oil*." Later – during the 50s? – it was delivered in bags which the haulage men humped straight to the bunker.

Unlike non-mining families, we never perceived coal as being rare or expensive. Fortunately the British Isles are geologically built on coal concentrated in the Scottish midlands, Geordieland, South Yorkshire, North Nottinghamshire and Wales boyo. Brave men, called miners, descended into the dark, damp, fetid bowels of the earth and ripped the coal out of the richest seams. Seams at the face might be as low as three feet high and the colliers worked on their knees shovelling relentlessly to keep the Empire great and their families fed and warm. The roof was supported by wooden beams which creaked all the time under the weight of the earth. If the beams ever stopped creaking the miners ran (crawled) like hell for the beams were about to snap.

To get to the coal face miners had to go down the shaft in a lift cage and walk maybe a mile underground and the roof would get closer and closer to the floor. Most men in Britain would not even have been able to walk to the face never mind work at it for seven hours. A mining area was always dominated by a tower with two big wheels, which was the lift over the pit shaft, and also by slag heaps – small mountains of rock and waste – also known as the Black

Alps. "Where there's muck there's brass, lad! Nowt wrong wi' that!"

Miners were a breed apart. They wore grey suits with baggy trousers and a cloth cap and a striped shirt with no tie and a muffler and usually had a fag in their mouth. They were cheerful down-to-earth men for the most part. Since pit-head baths had been installed in the late 40s they came home clean but before then they came home black with coal dust and had to bathe in front of the fire.

They liked to go to the pub at the weekend and drink pint after pint and smoke fag after fag and laugh. At night they went with their wives who sat by them contentedly sipping a Babycham or "gin and it" and kept their mouths shut as a woman should when she's with her man and let the men do all the talking. They liked music with Albert on the piano and Cecil on the drums. On special occasions they danced all the old waltzes and quicksteps and Knees up Mother Browns, a culture which held an Empire together. Drinks waiters had to anticipate the moves of the dancers so that they could dash between them without getting the tray knocked out of their hands.

If a miner went drinking without his wife he had to remember to go home in time for dinner. If he should forget, the pub might well be treated to the sight of an indignant housewife come charging through the door with a steaming plate, slam it on the table in front of her husband "If you won't come home for it, you'll just have to eat it here!" And she'd storm out while her husband smiled sheepishly around the room and asked the barman for some salt.

Such was a culture and a civilisation and an empire soundly founded on coal. It even had a special place in New Year festivities. If you were to have a happy new year you had to be **_first footed_** by a tall dark handsome man (sorry folks - not a miner!) coming through your door on the stroke of midnight with, in his hand, a lump of coal which he placed on your fire: "Happy New Year!"

Brian McGarrigle 1954-58
Santa Monica, California

CHAPTER 5

Anecdotes

A miscellaneous assembly of memories, comments and asides which do not neatly fit within the main chapters of the History.

Miss Todd First Senior Mistress

Miss Todd was determined to teach us good manners. On the first day of school she gave a demonstration on how to use a knife, fork and spoon – and often appeared in the dining room, checking our style!

Bill Bishop

Miss Todd was tall and slim – a Miss Brodie type. We were nearly all from humble homes but from families which had great hopes for us. Miss Todd certainly wanted the best for her girls.

Doris Marks

She insisted on clean fingernails and spotless uniforms. She delegated older girls (no prefects before 1944/45) to make spot checks as girls left the cloak-rooms on their way to class.

Kathleen Gibson

She obtained a doctorate and later became principal of Hull Municipal

Training College – still keen on table manners.

Gill Bunting

Dedication Service: 9 Oct 1939

I remember on that occasion a County Council dignitary told us that at council meetings PJGS was always referred to as *'Lane's Baby'*, referring to Alderman J W Lane of the West Riding County Council.

The Rev Taylor, of Adwick church, was invariably asked to propose the vote of thanks on Speech Days etc and on at least two occasions, which may have included the Dedication Service, he began by saying: *"I won't give you the speech I had prepared"*, ostentatiously pocketing a large sheaf of papers. The implication was that the preceding speeches had been far too long. He would then deliver an even lengthier vote of thanks. How long it might have been if he had used the notes, God knows!! His opening phrase became a standing joke amongst pupils and staff.

Dennis Smith

The Aero Café, Great North Road

Some of us may have wondered why the Aero Transport Café at the Redhouse service area was so called. Roy Jackson, who used to live in Woodlands, remembers his father taking him, around 1933, for Sunday morning walks along the A1 where for a long time, the old quarry by the service area housed a trailer that carried a large seaplane, which he believes was one of the two record-breaking Supermarine S6B planes. He never found out why it was there, and it disappeared by about 1939.

Roy Jackson

Velda Johnson (joined 1949) confirms that the Aero Café and adjacent houses were built by her grandfather and named after the parked aeroplane, which had been removed before her family went to live there around 1941. (IMN)

Before Pit-head Baths

Before showers were installed at the pits, at various times in the 40s, miners used to return from work in their dirt and bathe at home – often before the fire in a zinc bath. The hot water for this operation was sometimes prepared in a cast iron cauldron in the kitchen corner, called, perversely, " t' copper" which had its own little fire grate. This was also where the more grubby clothes were boiled with soda on Mondays, filling the kitchen with steam. The only detergent in those days was soap flakes, and the other laundry was done by hand in a zinc tub, agitated with a contrivance resembling a three-legged stool on a staff, called a "Peggy" or "Dolly". Mondays were days of hard work for the housewife. (– but lunch was easy since it was the leftovers from Sunday. KC)

Roy Jackson

Crab-apple Fights

If there are still *Splat!* marks with juicy trails beneath them on one of the lower classroom blackboards, that's where Form 4 Q in the early 40s had its crab-apple fights. We found that chalk dust made the marks virtually permanent.

Our working up a good fog by banging together well-loaded board erasers was something that piqued Mr Quine a bit.

Roy Jackson

Coal Fires – Draw-Tin

Re coal fires: There was also the Draw-Tin as an aid to hastening fire-lighting. This was a piece of sheet steel with a handle on the outer surface and a couple of hooks on the other. It was so sized that it covered the fireplace opening and supported a newspaper so as to seal the draught to top and sides and direct it from beneath the grate. This device was also handy as a shield in sword-fights - just as the coal rake made a great street hockey stick – roller skate games would rage along the whole street!

Roy Jackson

"Wonderful" Mr Field

One day (c 1944) I was sent on an errand. I've no idea now what it was about, but I had to go from from an upstairs classroom to somewhere downstairs. Since there was no-one else about I succumbed to the temptation of sliding down the bannister (absolutely forbidden behaviour*). As I

---

* Infringement of School Rule 1… **"Walk** on the left…." KC

reached the bottom Mr Field came round the corner. As you can imagine, I was terrified. I couldn't think what punishment might be deemed appropriate. Mr Field looked at me for what seemed ages. He then said "I wouldn't do that again if I were you, Kathleen" and walked away.

I always did like him…after that I thought he was wonderful!

Kathleen Gibson

Bunking Off - Mollie Peet vs Fanny Banks, Senior Mistress

In my time in the sixth form (mid 40s) we were very much left to our own devices, but there were a couple of individuals who had stayed on and were not taking exams. These people would hang around just waiting for a good gossip – not conducive to serious study. I developed a habit of bunking off early to work at home, but one day I was summoned to Fanny Banks's study where she told me I had been seen in town before 4 pm. I assured her she must be mistaken, that I must have a doppelgänger.

She looked me firmly in the eye and told me she would get me sooner or later. She didn't like me much – I can't think why. Anyway I instructed various younger girls to keep an eye out and one day one of them came to warn me just as I was about to leave the school premises and informed me that Fanny demanded to see me immediately in her study. I did so, wide-eyed and innocent. She was pretty cross, but there was nothing much she could do.

Mollie Peet

Fruit Picking in 1944

Miss Banks organised   a visit to a camp near Somersham in Huntingdonshire. She and Miss Grey accompanied a group of senior girls. (What an adventure! – I had never travelled further south than Chesterfield.) Some of us took our bikes on the train – we cycled to Ely on our free day together with Miss Grey. Ladders were used in the orchards to pick plums. When the ladders needed to be moved we called   for the foreman, Bob. He seemed elderly but was probably about 50! Health & Safety regulations in our current 'nanny' state would make an expedition such as this a 'non-starter'.

A group of girls from Watford were also in the camp. Miss Banks used to come to our tent in the evenings for a chat. I well remember her relating that she had overheard one of our party telling a Watford girl (in a strong South Yorkshire accent) that "We don't talk Yorkshire"!

We were able to send a box of fruit home and for several years afterwards my family received a large box of plums (by post) from Bob. Mum duly sent him a £1 note (or was it ten shillings?) The fruit was a rare treat!

Mary Hart

Little & Good

Mr Quine, a kind and generous man, became my form teacher when I transferred (1942) from another school. As I was new, he detailed two other girls in the form to look after me. One of these was a small and very perky little girl who initiated me immediately into the ethos of Percy's. I was tall and thin as a broomstick, with the lack of self-confidence that affects all freaks. She instructed me how to cope with the inevitable teasing: "If they have a go at me, I just say 'I am little and good', so you will have to say ' I am bigger and better'. Don't mind about it – they don't mean anything." She was quite right, there was no malice in my new school mates.

Mollie Peet

Dr Tennenhaus

Dr T came (c 1943) to live near us in Doncaster and became a friend of the family. As a Jew himself, it was he who first made us aware of what was going on under the Nazis in Europe. His wife and small son disappeared into the death camps and were never heard of again. He escaped from Vienna, where he taught history at the university, and was interned in Britain as an enemy alien before being cleared and joining the Pioneer Force.

His daughter Ruth was rescued by the Red Cross and eventually sent to Norway; but when the Nazis reached there she was trekked with other Jewish children across to neutral Sweden. The Red Cross eventually reunited her with her father in England and she became a pupil at Percy's. She later married a rabbi (R Gaguine), but unfortunately died at a rather young age.

Mollie Peet

Ruth's time in Norway explains how she obtained a pass in Norwegian in her School Certificate. (Prize Giving programme 14 March 1946) KC.

Northern Dairies Depot

The Milk Marketing Board maintained a quality control laboratory within the Northern Dairies depot, near the school's Tenter Balk Lane gate, and in the 40s senior boys would stroll across to chat with (or up?) the young ladies who worked there and possibly scrounge a cup of tea, a cigarette – even a glass of milk.

Dennis Smith & Roy Jackson

"Just getting our ball, Miss."

Head Boy in 1946/47 was Ernie "Titch" Roberts - who was quite short. He and a group of boys were playing football on the playground and Titch kicked the ball onto the roof of the gym changing room. He duly climbed onto the roof to recover the ball and paused to look through the skylight into the girls' changing room. The girls were unfortunately in the nude having come out of the shower and, even more unfortunately for Titch, the girls' gym teacher happened to look up as he looked down. The outcome was that poor Titch had to make a public apology to the entire school at next morning's assembly.

Michael Jackson

(Roy Jackson reports that precisely the same offence was committed in 1943 by a lad named Womack, but his punishment was a week's suspension.)

Masarella Ice-cream

Roy Jackson remembers Jeff Brooks in the 40s driving a horse and cart, peddling ice-cream for one of the Masarella brothers. This was a regular source of summer employment for generations of Percy's pupils – selling ice-cream or working in Masarella's dairy or their stables in Bentley and Arksey. By the 50s, sixth formers with a driving licence could even take command of a Masarella's van.

Not having a driving licence, Ken Cooke sold ice-cream around 1956 from horse-drawn carts for one summer season – and one season was quite enough! The horses were rotated from day to day and one had to learn to manage the foibles of each beast. Not one of them was normal or well-behaved.

"Paranoid ponies" is his enduring memory. Some would always want to turn in the opposite direction. Some couldn't pass a piece of green without stopping for a nibble. Short-legged "Dolly" really preferred to be stationary, which was a certain challenge when we needed to cross the A1 Great North Road at Sunnyfields – and this was before the Doncaster by-pass was built!

Ken's prayers seemed finally answered when he was allocated a large grey called "Major" for the Carcroft and Skellow round. Major was both placid and obedient – until home-time that is. Once it turned five o'clock and we turned to face Bentley, Major would abandon obedience and gallop all the way home along the A19! It scared the stuffing out of me. Phew!

Ken Cooke

Grand Cycling Club

In the 4th Form 1953, Cyril Storer, Arthur Parry and I were firm friends and enthusiastic cyclists. One day we decided we wanted to form a club, and decided we needed a president. We thought it only polite to ask our form master, Mac McChrystal, to assume that role and we duly arranged a meeting with him outside class hours. There sat Mac behind his big desk, and we three keen club-members in front of him.

"Sir, we are forming a club called 4AL Wheelers, and we would like you to be the president." "How many members do you have?" he asked.

To which we replied, nervously, "Er, there are just the three of us - for the present."

I can still see Mac's slightly amused smile, as he pondered for a few seconds how to get out of it. Then: "Well, I suggest you come back when you've got some more members, and we'll talk about it again."

We three kept on pedalling, without forming a club and without Mac - and our membership never increased.

David Pulman

Party after the Play

In 1955 I was stage manager for the school play (the one after Richard III). I had asked Chas if we could have a post-play party. Miss Dent refused to let the girls attend. I appealed to Chas to overrule this, which he did, adding: "But no alcohol Gravil." This I accepted - but somehow ignored.

After the performance we were in his study, which was habitually used as the boys' make-up and changing room, when one of the Ward brothers (I think it was Pete who was a friend of Les Holmes) crashed two bottles of cheap red wine together. It went all over that lovely Chinese green carpet – do you remember it? I spent all Sunday in a panic, expecting, at best, a caning, and at worst, expulsion. When I saw Chas on the Monday morning I was in a terrible state but all he said was "It needs cleaning, Gravil. Organise it." I had to collect two shillings and sixpence from all participants. This was a large amount in those poor days, but it paid for the cleaning. How wise and understanding Charlie was!

Geoff Gravil 1948-56

Craven 'A' Cork-tipped

One lunchtime (c 1954) Stanley and I were in the toilets together for a crafty smoke. I lit up and passed my fag packet under the next door for Stanley who then lit up. We were commenting expertly on the brand, when a voice boomed "What's going on? Who is smoking in there?" "Bl...y hell!.. It's Cockroft!" I murmured....."Nobody, Sir." I replied.
"OUT, OUT, OUT!" he ordered.
Stanley and I flushed our cigs down the toilet and came out.
"I know you've been smoking" says Cockroft "I can smell cigarette smoke yards away."
"Oh yes, a fitness fanatic like you probably could" I thought to myself.
"We haven't been smoking, Sir. Search me. I have no cigarettes on me."
"Don't lie to me boy; you have been smoking in this toilet. LOOK!" and, with my head shoved nearly down the pan, I observed a fag end bobbing about on the water. The game was up. We had been smoking "Craven A". Yes, they were cork-tipped and you could not flush them down a toilet.

We were hauled to Mr Elliot's office – to face the usual steely grey-blue eyes. "I'm going to cane you Parkin. This time a letter to your parents too." At home I received a lecture from my mother on the severity of the crime and the dreaded warning "Wait while your father comes in!" My Dad came home and much to my relief he was more amused than annoyed. I have not touched a "Craven A" since.

Tony Parkin 1949-55

Revenge on the Lower Sixth

It was about 1955/56 when the Lower Sixth stole into our Upper Sixth room and hung all the pictures upside down.   In retaliation, our chemistry A-level candidate (who **was** he?) smeared crystals of malachite green in Vaseline under the front edges of several desks in the Lower VI room. Result - bright green finger ends on some of the folks for days.

Jo Huddleston 1948-56

Atomic Pile

George Horsfield taught maths to the Science 6th in which I was from 1955 to 58. He was serenely effortless in all he did. A class consisted in us working through examples from the text book while he contemplated the universe. If we got stuck he'd sit by us and do the solution on our jotter."Ah, yes. P = mf." This magical equation was always the answer and he would solve it from there.

He was also a house master and was *supposed* to organize sports. In practice he just delegated everything to Big 'Ep (George Hepplestone).

Bob Steedman used to steal the chalk and lock it in a small cupboard labelled "Atomic Pile". George would come in to start the class and would look in vain for chalk. Then he'd turn round. "Steedman! Could I have some chalk please?"; "Yes sir, I'll see what I have." Bob would open the atomic pile which held a huge pile of new chalk and old. He'd pick a crummy little piece. "Here you are, Sir." George would accept it and spend the whole lesson with this titchy piece. I never understood why he put up with it.

When we left school in 1958, on the last day Bob wrote in big white letters on the windscreen of George's car P = mf.

Brian "Mac" MacGarrigle

Hound Dog

One Christmas circa 1957 we were allowed to use the assembly hall to play records. Mr Horsfield stepped in to take a short cut across the hall (which pupils were not allowed to do) just as Elvis screamed *"**You ain't nothing but a hound dog!**"* George visibly cringed - he had never heard rock and roll before as it was quite new. It was the only time I ever saw him walk quickly.

Brian McGarrigle

That Little Bit Extra

One day in 1957 when we were waiting to take the A-level Pure Maths exam in the library I was shocked to find that our maths teacher "Pansy" (Mrs Pamela Land) was outside offering us all a drink of Lucozade. She said that it would give us more energy! I felt sure that this must be against the exam rules set by the Northern Universities Joint Matriculation Board. What about all those poor kids whose teacher just allowed them water? Wasn't this a bit like a trainer doping the gee-gees before an important race? But "Thank you, Pansy".

Brian McGariggle

We all passed, so we sent a letter to Lucozade informing them. They asked if they could use the story for publicity, but on consideration we decided against. They did however send us some free samples.

Anne Limbert

Mother's Boy

I think Mr Rudd felt I was too much cosseted by my mother. One day c 1953 at the Woodlands church youth club he said "Give my love to your mother." When I next saw him he asked if I had given his love to mother. "Yes" I said "and she returns it." "Do you mean she reciprocates?" he asked. "No," I shot back "She returns it. She does not want it." I have to admit I meant "reciprocates" and it was not in my youthful nature to be so resilient. For a rare occasion it did silence Mr Rudd – no doubt he extracted revenge later.

Geoff Gravil

Mr Rudd called me "Uncle"

I don't know why Mr Rudd picked on me – I know I was tall and flat-footed. He nabbed me, on separate occasions, for my foul-smelling plimsolls and for my roll-neck jumper. It was on account of that jumper he called me "Uncle". Did he mean I was old for my years? Or was it just because he had to look up to me? Over time he sent me for the cane or detention more than any other teacher.

Brian "Wally" Wallwork 1950-54

A Stage Death

Mr Rudd played the lead in Shakespeare's "Richard II" in the local repertory company's performance at Doncaster Arts Centre, May 1955. A group of 5th formers attended, and three of us managed to get thrown out for applauding the "murder" of Mr Rudd.

Roy "Crum" Cromack 1950-57

The Inevitability of Nothingness

"Sid" Rudd was supervising a detention I was privileged to attend. He instructed us to write an essay on the "Inevitability of Nothingness". I produced a title and a blank sheet. If you are still out there Donald, please tell me what you expected.

Dave Etchell, 1956-1961

Death in the Classroom c 1953

"Baggy" Hanson (French teacher) was wont to clout boys around the head with whatever came to hand. On one such occasion, Mick St John, a hulking brute of a lad, pretended to drop down dead, and we all rushed over and declared she'd killed him, as he had a weak heart. She ran from the class in tears. We were a rotten lot!

Malcolm Palmer

Good Advice from Mac

Mr McChrystal impressed me with his pragmatism: "Since we are are all required to be in school, we may as well get something out of it."

Brian Wallwork

Red Herring

Mr McChrystal once c 1952 arrived for a Latin class with his foot bandaged. Facetiously, I asked if he had broken his foot. Quick as a flash – rehearsed for cheeky pupils like me, I suspect – he snapped "Gravil, I want a hundred lines from you, written alternately in red and black ink: 'It is incumbent upon me to refrain from drawing herrings of a crimson hue across the Latin trail.' " What a star!

Geoff Gravil

Can I go in with you, Mister?"

Cowboy films at the cinema could be "Adult" rated so children had to be accompanied. This was never a problem – at the ticket office we simply asked the next adult "Can I go in with you, Mister?" Imagine doing that today! It's not even politically correct.

Brian Wallwork

Cross-Country Run

There was a spell c 1953 when I couldn't do PE and when Mr Ron Cockroft was setting the boys off on the cross-country he would say "Shaw, can I borrow your bike?" and when they had set off he would say "I'm not going to follow them, but they will think I am!" But he sometimes did, because I remember once a group of us had called in at the Aero Café when Ron came along on his own bike. Oops!

I remember after I'd run in the Yorkshire Championships, Ron collared me on the Monday morning and said "Congratulations! I was reading the Yorkshire Post and saw that you finished second in the 880 yards." Was he perhaps just as proud as me?

Harry Shaw

Wally Wallwork made some awful groan-inducing jokes. On a cross-country he would say: "Darn it! I've got stitch."

Roy Cromack

On the cross-country we sometimes came across funeral parties at the cemetery on Red House Lane. One day in early 1958 it was almost impossible to negotiate our way through a very large gathering on the road outside. It was the funeral of Manchester United's left winger, David Pegg, who had died in the Munich Air Crash (6 Feb 1958).

John Roberts

Algie

Mr Cunnington, nickname Cunno or Algie, used to come to school on his motorbike from Sheffield, wearing goggles and a leather helmet. I guess that's why we called him Algie – he looked like Biggles's aviator friend. He used to write maths puzzle books. He wasn't good at discipline but if he lost his temper he could get really annoyed. I remember him hitting someone on the back of the neck and bursting a carbuncle for them.

Once we went to play De La Salle Grammar School at football in Sheffield. He met us at the bus station in Sheffield and took us to get a tram to the school playing field. When we stated our destination the conductor tried to charge us full fare but Mr. Cunnington stood up and said we were a school party and that we were only paying half fare. A row ensued but Cunno stood his ground and won.

Harry Shaw

Cunno liked to open lessons with "Now, if we take a young triangle…" and he would draw a small triangle on the board.

As punishment in detention he would have you copy out – maybe two or three times – a maths A-level scholarship exam paper, which was a mass of symbols and Greek letters.

Brian McGarrigle

At the first sign of a cold or 'flu Cunno would nip into the chemistry lab and take a good sniff from the 880 ammonia bottle – "to clear the tubes."

John Roberts

Miss Dent – Kinder than mother?

My mother had been brought up in the slums of Teesside and her parents couldn't afford to send her to grammar school when she "passed the scholarship" in the early 1920's. Consequently, she was determined I should have a first class education and therefore I was never allowed to miss school, even with illness. She would think I was putting it on.

When I was going through the inevitable changes of adolescence in 1954, I used to have the most awful stomach cramps but to her that was no reason to stay at home.

My friends, however, took pity on me and either Gloria Long or Christine Gray would take me along to Miss Dent. She gently probed as to why I came to school on these days and, when I explained, she told me I was not to hesitate to come to her again. I had expected her to have the same attitude as my mother but every month she would make me a hot water bottle and put me to bed. A wise and kind lady.

We girls had little contact with Chas but one day he caught me wearing my indoor shoes in the playground. I was mortified! But he simply instructed me to go inside and change into my outdoor shoes and nothing more was said.

Carol Pearson

Miss Malteser

I am not allowed to disclose her real name, but on her last lesson with us this young teacher read us parts from Lady Chatterley or Fanny Hill and brought a box of Maltesers to share with the class. She had Barry Seymour and me sit at the front with her and kept giving us extra Maltesers. She would probably get reported nowadays for sexual harassment.

At one Christmas party she said to me "Why aren't you as shy as this in class?" and asked me to dance with her – a real punishment for me in those days.

Harry Shaw

Bulls' Eyes Pass over if you're squeamish (c 1953).

Remember dissecting cows' eyes in biology class? (This in the voice of 'Jake' Jevans:) "Do you know where they came from? Well, I will tell you… I discovered that Cooke passed through town on his way home, so I arranged for him to call at the abattoir by the cattle market and collect some." And it was quite an experience. The manager was expecting me and had his foreman lead me through the bloody hides and gore and offal to this pile of eyeballs: "Help youself, lad. Know how many you need?"

Ken Cooke

"Don't Call Me Miss!"

Miss Molly Marsden (RE) put the fear into us. If you called her "Miss" she would either ignore you or say "I've got a handle to my name. Use it."

Mrs Severn (English), a very respected member of staff, insisted that boys touched their caps when they saw her out of school. She was another teacher who didn't like to be called Miss. "I am not a Miss. My name is Mrs Severn." She and her husband had the Post Office at St. Martins Avenue on York Road.

She could be very sarcastic. The day after I won the school cross-country she said: "Shaw, you nearly gave me a heart attack yesterday." "How was that, *Mrs Severn*?" I asked, and she said "Winning yesterday - because you are nearly always last to my lessons."

Harry Shaw

The Phantom Fair-Isle Knitter

Margaret Pidcock asked recently if it was Clive Roberts who shamed the lower sixth girls with his expertise at Fair-Isle knitting (c 1956). Clive has admitted that it was indeed he. His mother taught him to knit whilst he was confined to bed with measles.

Miss Hilda Beal

Miss Beal tended to open geography lessons with "The world is round. Its axis is tilted at twentythree and a half degrees to the perpendicular. If it were not so, there would be no seasons and day and night would be of equal length. Do you understand that? Thank you."

She also swore to give up teaching if I passed o-level history. I did, and she didn't, but I don't know what that proves. (- That she was a very good motivator? KC)

Malcolm Palmer

Miss Beal was clearly better trained in the classics than we were. In her geography lessons when we didn't follow Latin phrases or English derivations from Latin she would explode: "Don't you know **any** Latin?". The irony was that, for time-tabling reasons, those of us taking Geography from the third form had to forgo Latin.

Margaret North

The 4th year science stream around 1954 used to suffer boring dictation from the history teacher. For relief, they would sometimes check in the textbook and tell "Miss" she had made a mistake, to which she would unfailingly retort "*The book is wrong!*".

In a lesson dealing with the contortions of Italian states, Palmer had managed to doze off. With extra emphasis on the important bits, Miss launched onwards with "**Parma**, **Modena and Tuscany**..." On hearing his name called, Palmer instantly revived and extemporized an answer to a supposed question – much to the puzzlement of the teacher and to the amusement of his classmates.

Roy Cromack

Robbo's Skiffle Group 1956/57

John "Robbo" Robinson (1950 entrant) had always had a very good voice. He appeared as a soprano on Wilfred Pickles's "Have a Go" radio programme, presented from Woodlands Welfare Hall, on the BBC around 1951: "Give 'em the money, Barney!" Around 1956 with the inspiration of Lonnie Donegan and the attraction of cheap instruments, he formed a skiffle group

Ken Cooke

The group featured Robbo as lead guitar and vocalist, Les Holmes on tea chest bass, Clive Roberts or alternatively Norman "Wainy" Wainwright on second guitar and Barry Paddock washboard–percussion. Apart from school functions, the group played at pubs and clubs around Doncaster and even earned some money! Their titles were all Donegan: Rock Island Line, Last Train to San Fernando, Cumberland Gap and Digging My Potatoes. (Not My old Man's a Dustman – that came later).

The group wound down when headmaster Elliott called them in and said they ought to choose between performing and academic progress. (Clive became a dentist and Norman an electrical engineer. KC)

Clive Roberts & Norman Wainwright

Robbo was a Card

Robbo was quite a card. Outgoing, a performer and a dedicated believer in fun – not to mention tall and good looking – he inevitably got into many scrapes. He was the first boy in school to abandon the short back and sides haircut and one day in 1955 appeared with a "Tony Curtis" coiffure. This style, along with the crew-cut and the semi-crew, became essential badges of the pop music culture.

Ken Cooke

In the school library there was a fireplace which was never used for a fire. Robbo would drape himself across the hearth, facing up the chimney, to smoke a cigarette. The fumes would go up the chimney and not be detected in the library. He would often drink his school milk in the library and stash the empty third-pint bottles behind books on the shelves.

Another trick he had with school milk was to uncrimp the foil top, invert the bottle on top of the library clock and then carefully slide out the foil. This left a full bottle, without a cap, upside down on the clock. Clearly nobody was eager to chance removing it, so it was left to nurture penicillium and goodness knows what other moulds. These bottles remained there for a very long time and I don't know which brave soul finally removed them. Could they still be there?

Brian McGarrigle

A Musical Lunch
One fine summer's lunchtime c 1957 three or four sixth formers ambled down the field to the Forester's Arms. As usual everyone began to hang back as we approached the door of the pub. We went in and saw the usual array of local worthies staring into space and making a half last for an hour. We got equipped with pints when Robbo noticed the piano. He sat down and began to play and to sing, whereupon the elderly regulars came alive and their eyes began to gleam. So a good time was had by all. A wonderful example of bridging the generation gap, which Chas would surely have been proud of – had he been there to witness it.

The others and I realized it was time to get back to school and left but Robbo was having such fun he stayed behind. We walked up over the field and back to school. I had to take my homework to a teacher in the staff room. I knocked and went in and presented the teacher with my homework. As he began to look at it I noticed that the windows were wide open and realized that the sound of a distant piano borne on the summer breeze was wafting quite clearly through the window.

Then the teacher asked: "Where's Robinson? He's supposed to give me his work too."

"I don't know, Sir!" – "Hmmph!"

I thought "If only you knew that the piano you can hear right now is coming from the village pub and is being played by Robbo!"

Brian McGarrigle

Every Good Boy Deserves Favour?

Around 1956 class 1B was having a basic music lesson with Mr Mayman and he was checking that we knew the letters for the notes: "What are the notes on the lines?" he asked. " E G B D F" someone volunteered. "Very Good". Frank Bradshaw, who was more interested in football, was not paying much attention. Mr M next asked "Bradshaw, what are the notes in the spaces?" Bradshaw, perplexed, looked to his colleagues and I tried to help by pointing at my f.a.c.e. Quick as a flash, he replied to teacher "D I A L , Sir". We all had a good laugh, including Sir.

John Roberts

I wish I'd never done it!

Going home on the school bus around 1958, I had naughtily pinched a magazine from one of our girl classmates. But woe!... Mr Cockroft happened to board the same bus. He noticed – and made jolly sure that I knew he had noticed – that I was reading the girls' comic "Mirabelle". From the next day onwards he referred to me by my new nickname of "Mirabelle". I felt so taunted. I wish I'd never done it!

Bernard Warner 1956-61.

SOS on the Flagpoles : "Save Our Smalls".

Following the annual senior school dance, generations of male pupils recall hoisting items of female underwear up the flagpoles over the school frontage. It was a tradition.

Many old boys. Memory prompted by Bernard Warner.

The Honourable Member for Rotherham

Mr O'Malley (history 1959-61) looked strict and was strict, but he was more interested in music and politics than teaching, I suspect. He played in a dance band and often got back very late, the result being that he could sometimes be tired at school. Once, having set the class individual work, he fell asleep across his desk and one by one all the pupils tip-toed out of the classroom! He went on to become Labour MP for Rotherham.

(Sleeping in the House of Commons is OK? KC)

Janet Kitson

All for One & One for All

It was during a maths lesson in a laboratory in the science block around 1960 and Mr Beevers was busy writing on the board. We were seated at the benches which were fitted with porcelain sinks overarched with tall taps. In readiness for the next chemistry lesson, each tap was fitted with a length of rubber tubing. James Marshall, a mischievous lad with a roguish smile, could not resist turning on a tap – slowly at first and nothing happened. So he opened it some more ... and some more and *suddenly* the tube burst into life, whipping round and spraying water everywhere – including the blackboard which now looked as if some large dog had cocked a leg at it.

A slightly wet Mr Beevers turned and joined in the laughter momentarily, before enquiring "Who did that?" Well, as every Piglet knows, it is taboo to snitch on a colleague and so the whole class was given detention. Still, it was well worth it just to see the shock on Marshall's face.

Janet Kitson

The Path to Heaven?

Molly Marsden instructed us to write out the Lord's Prayer in our exercise books. She read mine out to the class, as I had written "Our Father we chart in heaven..." Then she asked me "What are you going to do, lad, go to heaven and make a map?"

In one of her history lessons I wrote "The Medes suffered a tax from the Persians". It should have read "attacks". Molly was not amused.

Derek Jones: left 1959

Tent Pegs – Only 4d

One of the exercises Mr Pilsworth set in woodwork class in the early 60s was making a tent peg. When completed we could buy these for 4 old pence each – but what use is a single tent peg? Most lads didn't bother, which suited Mr P since he was scout leader and the pegs could be used at camp. I bought mine out of spite.

John Smurthwaite

The Western Roll for Six

I will always remember (c 1967) coming out of the dining hall, running across the playground and practising my Western Roll high jump over the large privet hedge. Unfortunately, I landed on the school caretaker, working on his vegetable patch. He must have reported me, for later in the day I was hauled out of Miss Marsden's class by none other than the head, Mr Atherfold, who gave me six of the best – including two for my wearing orange socks!

David Clarke

Four Generations – Three School Names

My uncle, Ken Pidcock, was at Percy's 1942-49, leaving just before I joined in 1950 until 1956. My children Derek, Sandra and Philip Burns attended between 1980-85, when it was Adwick School, the comprehensive, and my youngest grandson started in 2002. It is now called North Doncaster Technology College (NDTC).

Margaret Pidcock Burns

Conclusion

"We live in interesting times." At the Percy Jackson Grammar School we certainly did, and it seems to me that the pupils - Percy's Piglets - contrived to make things yet more interesting. The first head, Mr Field, with the responsibility of establishing the new school, had to cope with the complications of a world war whilst his pupils decorated their gas-masks and speculated on a romance between their teacher and the captain of a battleship. His successor, 'Chas' Elliott, was obliged to cram extra pupils into prefabricated buildings and to worry about high wages and Rock 'n Roll diverting pupils from staying on in the sixth form. And the last head, John Atherfold, was preparing to impose the comprehensive system on the more privileged, more up-front generation of the Baby Boomers.

Certainly, they were interesting times - at times exciting – but, more to the point, over its twenty-nine years the school succeeded in every way. The dedication and leadership of the staff, the industry of the pupils and a pervading positive ambience combined to produce successful outcomes for the thousands of young people who passed through Percy Jackson's. As Mr Cockroft asserted in his foreword to this History, the school did indeed provide for its pupils a solid base for a rewarding and satisfying adult life.

"Try so to live that you can always say that now is the best time of your life."
So Professor E B Castle counselled us on Speech Day, 6 November 1952 –
nearly halfway through the school's history. Yet how could schooldays be
the proverbial best days of our life when so much of life was yet to come?
Perhaps we should just accept – at the risk of lapsing into Shakespeare - that
each stage of life is different. Each has its own properties and its own
standards to be judged by. How do we compare the camaraderie of schooldays with being a doting grandparent? Well, I would say that each stage of
life has its own challenges, its own adventures and its own rewards.

Whether any stage is to be considered "good" or "the best" will depend on
the balance of benefits and enjoyment on the one side as against the sacrifices
and the obligations on the other. A large helping of adventure and fun can
easily tip the balance - and to those who didn't get their share at school, I
hope they caught up later.

To me – call me an über-romantic – joining Percy's was the beginning of an
era of adventure. I sincerely hope that some of my romanticism is reflected
in this work. Compiling the *History* has been another great adventure for
me. I have consulted sages and my noble peers. I have re-cast the runes,
untied ancient knots, re-wooed fair damsels and re-slain old dragons….. **You
all know which you are!**

Keep Troth!

Sources & Contributors
With Intake Year for former Pupils

BF: Barbara Fox (1939)

DC: David Cranshaw (joined 3rd form in1939)

DM: Derrick Moore (1939)

DS: Dennis Smith(1939)

RJ: Roy Jackson (1939)

MH: Mary (Hart) Hutchinson (1939)

WDB: William "Bill" Dennis Bishop (1939)

EO: Elizabeth "Betty" (Oates) Bishop (1939)

RH: Raymond Hide (1940)

NSS: Norman Staveley, Riley High School, Hull (1940)

DOM: Doris (Marks) Beeson (1940)

KRG: Kathleen (Gibson) Pumfrey (1940)

AHR: Audrey (Harrison) Roberts (1942).
      Daughter of Mr Harrison, metalwork teacher.

MJ: Michael Jackson (1943)

MPJ: Mollie (Peet) Jenkins. Joined 4th form in 1942.

JH: John Hudson (1946)

IMN: Margaret (North) Cook (1949) & research of School Records.

DNP: David Noel Pulman (1949)

RB: Bob Bentley (1949)

BBK: Barbara (Brooks) Knight (1949).

GBG: Gillian (Bunting) Gravil (1949).

AL: Anne (Limbert) Stidwell (1950)

KC: Ken Cooke (1950): Compiler of the History.

MJP: Malcolm "Mick" Palmer (1950)

HS: Harry Shaw (1950)

MS: Margaret (Skinner) Griffiths (1950)

BMcG: Brian McGarrigle (joined 4th form in 1954)

CPE: Carol (Pearson) Edgar (1954)

GC: Glyn Court (teacher, German, French.1953-57)

JR: John Roberts (1955)

JKR: Janet (Kitson) Roberts (1959)

GB: George Brooks (Teacher, German 1956-68)

FJA: John Atherfold (Head 1966-68)

SM: School Magazine, "The Balkite" from 1959.

SR: School Records & Log Book (Doncaster Archives)

EB: Encyclopaedia Britannica 2001

Appendices

1   Teaching Staff

With their approximate dates of service.

1940s

Mr Ronald Field 1939-45: Physics. First Head.

Miss Hellena Todd 1939-42: First Senior Mistress.

Mr Victor Milson 1939-45: Maths & Senior Master, with an absence on military service.

Miss Mona Fell 1939- : German. A lively young teacher and modern in her approach. Miss Fell left PJGS for a job in London about the same time a number of us went to various London colleges. She gathered us at a soiree, with Derrick Hutchinson, Mary Hart, Buggy Burston, Joyce Reynolds, and I believe Kathleen Gibson, among others. She hoped to make this a regular affair, but it never came to pass, and that was the last I saw of her. She was an excellent teacher, and I've found my halting German most useful.(RJ)

Mr Belton (Art, Woodwork) went into the RAF about 1940. He was a fine artist, and a powerful cyclist.

Stella Price. Chemistry. Tall, athletic, and popular. Left about 1944.

Miss Johnson 1939-41?, Domestic science.

Mrs Cartledge 1939-42: Girls' PE.

Mr L C Johnson 1940-44: Science; Senior Master during Vic Milson's absence. A tall, lean disciplinarian. A good teacher who didn't suffer fools gladly – in fact he didn't suffer them at all. (RJ)

Mr Black 1940s: PE and maths.

Miss Betty Main: 1940s

Mr C Emmott: 1945-46: History & RI. "Fiery Emmott" with his bristly moustache. He was there for a year or so from probably 1940, until he was called up. He returned for a short while after the war, but soon left for a senior job elsewhere.

He was a stern but fair man, an excellent history teacher, open-minded examiner of the scriptures, a disciplined and enthusiastic chorus master. (RJ)

Miss Kathleen E Homan 1941-42: English, French. Appears to have acted as Senior Mistress for a short time.

"Miss Doreen" Homan 1940s: Sister of the above, joined later. Music?

Miss Evelyn Banks 1942-49: English. Senior Mistress 1942-49.

Miss Beati Havard-Jones 1942-45 : Physical Education. Had semi-shingle cut hair and always wore trousers, which made her the subject of suspicion from girls' mothers (DOM).

Miss Reynolds 1940- : Art. She probably took over when Belton was called up 1940.

Mr W "Bill" E Quine 1941-47: English. Famous for his puns. Hated sudden noises, from experience in the London blitz (DS). Leader of the school scout group soon after its foundation. A conscientious and caring man as well as a fine teacher, he didn't find controlling rowdies very easy. (RJ)

Miss Hobson 1939- : Maths - brought back from retirement to replace a teacher called up to the forces.She was not strong on discipline, it is said (BF). Whilst generally well-behaved, we were noisy and pestering in her classes.(DOM) She also had a degree in German, but preferred to teach maths, in which endeavour, if we listened, she was very good. She was a very heavy smoker.(RJ)

Miss Olga W Gray 1942-47: History. Small lady with hair in a bun. Conscientious, well organised. (DOM)

Miss K Anderson 1942- : Dom Science. Leader of school cubs. Boys started the first form at ten years old in the early days. Said to be engaged at one time to Mr John Good.

Miss Stewart (Mrs Fox)19..- 47: French. Left to join her husband in the USA.

Miss Biddick 1940-47: Geography. Brought back from retirement. Miss Biddick had been a missionary in India for years, and returned to the UK about 1943 or 44.(RJ)

Miss Houghton 19..-47: Geography, English?

Miss Hoyle 19..-47: German

Mr Bell 19..-47: Science. Primarily Biology. He initiated "Ecology Trips" to nearby countryside.

Miss Campbell 19..-45: Maths? or French, German?

Mr Ken D Rockett 1942-53: German, French. Exempt from call-up on health grounds. Went on to become a professor at Newcastle University.

Mr Harrison 1942-49: Metalwork and Technical Drawing. His children attended PJGS. Known as "Butch" the butcher, for sharpening kitchen knives when on dinner duty (AHR). Ran the school flight of the Air Training Corps.

Miss Hargreaves 1942- : Music, maths. Managed the school choir.

Miss Smith 1943-48: History, music. Good pianist. Assisted with the choir.

Dr Michael Tennenhaus 1943-55: German. The longest serving member of staff up to that time. (School Magazine 1955/56). Instigator of the 1953/54 exchanges with Germany. Nicknamed "Butch" as a mispronunciation of the German "Buch". (KC) See Chapter 5.

Mr John Good 1944-49: English. "Johnny Good". Founder of the School Magazine in printed format. Active in the Gramophone Club. Married former pupil, Peggy Ruddock.

Miss Duke 1944-47: Dom Sci

Miss Smith 1944- :History. "Young, glamorous and friendly" (KRG)

Mr Ken S Fletcher 1944-48: PE. He recruited as a volunteer soccer coach Syd Bycroft, ex professional with 17 seasons at Doncaster Rovers under his belt. Assisted with the running of the ATC.

Miss Mills 1940s: Latin.

Mr Rees 1948-49: R E

Mr W J Cunnington 1945-64: Maths and Senior Master. "Cunno" and "Algie". For many years commuted to school on a motorbike. Died in service after 19 years at Percy's.

Mr Cecil Elliott 1945-66: The second Head of PJGS. "Chas". 21 years service.

Mr Yarnold 1945-49: Physics. Leader of the school dance band. Ex-RAF, Cranston college. Good man.

Mr Hanmer 1946-1950: Geography."Happy Harry". Active supporter of the SCM.

Mr Wilkinson 1946-49: Chemistry. "Wilkie" had all the characteristics of a long-time bachelor, but he saved the day for those of us in the sixth form, as in 1945 good teachers were hard to come by.(RJ)

Miss Campbell 1946-49: French

Miss B M Massey 1946-52: Geography. Arranged school trips to Switzerland and retired there. Depending on their mood, boys would call her "Miss Massey with the classy chassis" or "Bossy Bessy" (MJ)

Mr W Pilsworth 1946-67: Woodwork. "Wilf". One of the longest serving teachers - 21 years. Loved or hated! "Now boys, gather round this bench"- either for a technical demonstration or for the public humiliation of a pupil. Wilf was a patient man, but had his limits. One boy's mortice & tenon frame was so abysmal that he wrapped it round the lad's neck. Not difficult, since the joints were so pathetically ill-fitting! The lad, a reputable ornithologist, now lives in

Spain. (KC).

Mrs Richardson 1947-56 Geography & History: "Spitfire" for her savage tongue towards miscreants.Mrs R had a vehement contempt for pupils whom she perceived were not pulling their weight. If it was a boy she would scold "Down the mine!That's where you belong."(KC) Remembered for her "vigorous and thorough teaching", she died in January 1957.

Miss E L Hanson 1947-60: French : "Baggy". Was quite free in clouting boys' heads, which may partly explain why she became a victim of the Blackboard Jungle culture (MJP/KC).

Miss Eleanor M Mayers 1947- : History. Did not understand 5AS's giggles at the mention of Garibaldi. Anne Limbert tried to explain it was the name of a biscuit, but Miss M still didn't see the humour! (HS) That really takes the biscuit!

Miss Stewart 1940s-47: (Mrs Fox) Left to join her husband in South America.

Mrs Inch 19..- 1950:

Miss Gill (later Mrs Firth) 1940s: PE

Miss Eileen M Crowe 40s/50s/60s : German. Make-up specialist for school plays.

Mr Reg W Greenwood 1947 -52: English.

Mr Joe Forrester 1946?-68..- : Art. Longest serving member of staff. A patient and gentle teacher who could always find something to praise. Died suddenly of a heart attack whilst mowing the lawn one weekend.(BBK)

Miss Williamson 1947-49: English. Young female teacher - popular with the boys.

Miss Rowlinson 1948-49 : Music, History.

Miss Wilson (Mrs Morton) 1948-53: PE

Mr A G Brown 1948-51: Maths. Supporter of the Gramophone Club.

Mr Ralph Scurfield 194. -55: Biology. "Dan", "Scurvy Dan". Said to have a nasty temper.

Miss D J Dent 1949-65 : Senior Mistress: English. Miss Dent's Detention "Fair and noble hostess, We are your guests tonight." Macbeth. School magazine 1949-50.

Mr Ernest J Powdrill 1949-53 : Physics. "Ernie" also "George". A tribute: "Throw Physics to the dogs: we'll none of it" – Macbeth. School Magazine 1949-50.

Mr Herbert Mayman 1949-68: Music, Maths. Senior Master 1964-68. Stalwart master of the choirs. One time cox for Cambridge in the Varsity boat race.

Mr W R F Cockroft 1949-68: PE & Games: "Ron" : Builder of character – although we didn't know at the time.Promoter of YHA walking holidays. Continued with the comprehensive until 1978.

Ron saw war service from 1939 to 1946. He was commisssioned in June 1940 as an officer in the Royal Armoured Corps. During 1944-45 his unit of Churchill tanks advanced from Normandy across the Rhine to the Ruhr. He was awarded the Military Cross in France in June 1944 and was demobbed in April 1946 in the rank of major. A "Boys' Own" hero.

Mr Alan Dixon 1949-68: Physics: "Deadshot Dixon" – accurate in throwing cricket balls – and pieces of chalk at unruly pupils. His standard greeting to the class was "Sit down and shut up!" He did a temporary teaching session in 1948 before joining the permanent staff. He saw war service with the army from 1944, spending three years in India and Egypt before being demobbed in November 1947 in the rank of captain. He stayed on at the comprehensive school until retiring in 1984, having spent his entire teaching career at the one site.

Mr John Milburn 1949-51 : Chemistry.

Mr Arthur McChrystal 1949-1957: Latin, History (French): "Mac". Had a wry sense of humour and a penchant for giving his own nicknames to his pupils: "Johnny B", "Young Cooky", "Miss Wright", "Flags" (for Gill Bunting), "Grandeur" for **A W**addoups (AWe). Today some of these might not be politically quite correct. (KC). Mac served in Burma during World War II.

Miss Burgess 1949-..: German.

Mrs Outram 1939-48: School Secretary

Miss D M Wood 1948- : School Secretary.

1950s

Miss Medley 1950-51 : English.

Miss Norton 1950-..: English.

Miss P O Lewin 1953-60 : P E : "Lulu". Girl pupils suspected she was a bad influence on Mr Cockroft (IMN). Boy pupils could see why (HS).

Miss J P Revill 19..- : Domestic Science

Mrs Pam Land (née Crisp) 1951-1965? Maths: "Pansy". Not just an excellent teacher of pure mathematics but also of ballroom dancing (BMcG).

Mr Hilton Clarke 1951 -1954: English. His sister was the well-known actress Jane Hylton (1927-79).

Mr Eric Ormandy 1949-56 : Metalwork (also Maths) "Taff". "Ruled with a rod of iron." An authority on the campaigns of Alexander. (SM 1956-57)

Mr Ken Muddiman 1950-60s : German & French.

Mr George E Horsfield: P=mf 1950s-60: Maths

Mr Bryn Coates 1951-53: Chemistry. A first class rugby player.

Mr John J Jevans 1953-68: Maths, Science. "Jake". Instilled on us scientific method – "Given, to prove, construction, proof" (MJP). Had a reputation for mood swings. On a good day he would enter the classroom singing a TV jingle like "It's a Heinz sooou-perday" (JKR). His attention often drifted into his open briefcase on the bench. Was it the Telegraph crossword or miniature chess?

Mrs K Severn 1952-60   English : "Kate" or "Purple Monster"- her favourite dress colour. Feared for her discipline, admired for her teaching skills. (KC and others)

Mr Donald R Rudd 1952- : English. "Sid" because he was not! (DNP). Used to give lines in unusual numbers, e.g. 27 or 33 (BMcG)

Miss Joyce Jones 19..-52 : Dom Sci (married teacher Mr Alan Dixon)

Miss Hazel Bilson 1951-63 : Dom Sci (ex-PJGS pupil & married ex-pupil Tony Waddoups). Hazel died in Oct 2000 and Tony died about a year later.

Mr Roy Groom 1951-52 : English. (married ex-pupil Gladys Hall)

Miss Gladys Bedford 1952 -1960: Domestic Science (Married Mr D Haigh)

Mr David Haigh 1953-60: Chemistry (married Miss Bedford). David died suddenly in 1964.

Miss M Marsden 50s-60s - Religious Instruction,History, Engl Lit: "Molly". She used to go round to George and Joyce Brooks to see "Dad's Army" on TV.(GB)
Her father was head at Carcroft junior school and quite a domineering person-ality (MJP).

Mr Barker 1952- : Geography.

Miss Hilda J Beal 50s-60s: History, Geography: "Hilda".

Mr Glyn Court 1953-57: German, French. "Lavrenti" after Beria (DNP).
In World War II Glyn saw active service in some of the famous river campaigns in Burma. He took part in the Battle of the Sittang Bend, 26-27 July 1945, the last action fought by any British batallion in the War. Glyn was the BBC's **Brain of Britain** in 1973.

Mr T Cox 1952-58 : Maths (former pupil of PJGS 1939-44) "Tom". Popular with boy pupils (MJP). Not surprising that Tom was popular: he was amiable, level headed and humorous, and was the senior pupil throughout his tenure, well deserving the role. He was a pretty good medium pace bowler, too. (RJ)

Miss Teal c 1951-54 : Geography. Our own "Sweater Girl."

Miss Fish 1954 - 56: Geography

Miss Bulmer 1953-56: History

Mrs Beaumont 1954-56: English

Dr Alan Eslick 1955- : Biology. "Plonk": Was always finding novel uses for his empty pipe-tobacco tins (Rich Dark Honeydew). His daughter Caroline was a pupil at Percy's.

Mr Arnold Wilson 1955-59: Biology: Used to ridicule pop music.

Mr George Brooks 1955-68: German, French. Active in the new wave of school travel, in promoting tennis and boys' hockey.

Mrs Joyce Brooks: late 50s-61: Geography (married to George Brooks).
Daughter Vicki was a PJGS pupil.

Mr W Graves 50s-1960: Music, Games.

Miss Hilary Le Fevre 58-1960: Art, Games.

Miss Hoult 1956- :

Mr John Groom 56-60s: Physics.

Mr Lawrence Egarr 56-67: Metalwork

Mr Firmin 1956-58 :

Miss Rita Bintcliffe 1956- : English: "Caesar adsum iam forte, sed Brutus passus sum".
(JR)

Mr Jones 1956- :

Mr Rothwell 1958-61 : Latin

Mr R (Bob) Oliver 1957-61and 1966-85: Geography. "River water upon entering an
estuary becomes saline by a series of imperceptible gradations." (Dave Etchell)

Mr Keith Brooks 1957- 60s: French

Mr Harrison 1957- :

Miss Deebank 1957-60: English, History.

Miss Neary 1957-58:

Mr John Beevers 1958- 62: Maths

Miss Swallow 1958-59:

Mr Graves 1958-60 :

Mr Foster 1958-61 : PE

Mr Craig 1959-61 : Biology

Miss Silverwood 1959-62 : English (former PJGS pupil).

Mr O'Malley 1959-61: History. Looked strict and was strict. (JKR)

1960s

Mr J R Davie 1962- : English. Model railway club

Miss Megan Farrar 1961-: PE (died fairly young of cancer)

Mr Jim Woodward 1961-68 : French - "M'sieur Woodward" and "Fidel".

Mr Binns 50s: Geography. Went on to a university post (professor).

Mr Dennis W Parrot 1962-66 : Art

Mr Mike Stables 1962..- : Librarian, English.

Miss Joan Williams 1963- : French. Used to bring in real French materials: magazines
& exercise books. Married Mr Stables.

Mr Sid Thrower 1961-67:Biology: Also known as "Percy Thrower". Organised YHA walking holidays. Well remembered for his constant smile – even when playing an Ugly Sister in the local panto.

Mrs Nancy (née Tagg) Micklethwait: 1961- : Domestic Science (former PJGS pupil).

Mr Jim Smith 60s: Physics.

Miss Hyde 19.. -61:

Miss Birley 1961-61 :

Mr David Robbie 61- : History also sports. Liked to wear his AAA tracksuit on the field. Married school secretary Anne Rowlands.

Mr Battye 1961- : Maths. Always wore a brown tweed suit with elbow patches.

Mr Jim Price 60s: Geography.

Mr Derek Harrison 60s: Chemistry, RE.

Mrs Davies 60s: Maths.

Mr Ted Fox 1961-64 : Maths, Games.

Mrs Beaumont 60s: History.

Miss Ebben 1961- :

Mr Chatterton 1961-61 : Music

Mr Gordon Johnson 1962- : Music. Dressed very smartly with polished black shoes.

Miss Rosemary Mead (Mrs Armstrong) 60s: Maths.

Mr Frankland 60s: French.

Mr Selwyn Rees 60s: Maths. (His father taught RE in the late 40s).

Miss Pat Irving 1962-64: Maths

Mr John Fay 1961- : Latin.

Mr John Melhuish 1962-: Geography. Sometimes dropped off to sleep whilst showing us slides.

Mr Derek Culley 60s-67: History.

Mr John Hoyle 1961-66 : Chemistry. Managed to put humour into experiments without compromising safety.

Mr Robinson 19..-61:

Miss Dearden 19..-63:

Miss Short 19..- 64:

Miss Sheila Chester 1961-64: PE (former PJGS pupil 1950-56). Sheila (married name Mosby) died in March 2000.

Mrs Holloway 1962-64 :

Mrs Leggard 1960s: Dom Sci

Mrs Cranswick 1960s: Dom Sci

Mr Jim Smith 1964-67 : Science

Miss Betty Rhodes 60s: English

Mr Sandland 60s-67:

Mr John Walton 60s-67:

Mr George Findlay 19..- 63: Economics, Russian

Miss Gail Goodwin 1966-: Art

Miss Cole 60s: PE

Mr Ken Langley 60s:

Mr Jones 1964-66: Economics & Games. Embezelled the money for the Italian skiing trip, 1966.

Mr Noel Senior 60s: Maths and Games. Drove a sports-modified Mini. Was once carried off the sports field with suspected heart attack – indigestion! (Steve Roberts)

Mrs Ann Holloway 19..- 64:

Margaret Conway 1964- : Maths

Miss Janet Newbert 1964- : Geography

Mr Ian Brameld 1964- : Maths.

Mrs Brooks 1964- : Geography, Games.

Mrs Johnson 1964- : English.

Mrs Sheila Wood 1965- : Senior Mistress.

Mr Weston 60s: Music. A demon with the blackboard rubber!

Mr John Atherfold 1966-68: The third and last Head of PJGS. Continued as Head of the comprehensive, the Adwick School, until 1988.

Miss Groom 19..-67:

Mrs Lund 19..-67:

Miss Moffatt 19..-67:

Mr Williams 1967- : Head of chemistry.

Mrs Hinchliffe 1967- : English

Miss Ashworth 1967- : Dom Sci

Mr Vic Seize 1967-: Metalwork.

Mr Cavill 1967- : Head of History & General Studies

Mr Gittins 1967- : Woodwork

Mr Ashwood 1967- : French, German.

Miss Baker 1967- : Science.

Miss Witherington 1967- : English.

Mr Edwards 1967- : English.

Mr Ogden 1967- : French, English.

Miss Owen 1967- : History.

Mr Hallgate 1967- : Boys PE

Miss Maguire 1967- : Girls PE

Mrs Alwood 1967- : Maths.

Mr Turner 1968- : Biology.

2. Scholarship Awards

1946	2	1951	5	1956	4	1961	12
1947	4	1952	7	1957	13	1962	16
1948	3	1953	14	1958	12	1963	16
1949	1	1954	7	1959	9	1964	16
1950	2	1955	8	1960	8	1965	33

These figures do not reflect the full extent of pupils going on to higher education since, in the 40s and 50s, possibly double these numbers went on to Teacher Training Colleges, where grants were funded under a separate system. In the later 60s it became the practice that all aspiring teachers took a degree.

3. Head Boys & Head Girls.

Year	Head Girl	Head Boy
1942-44	Iris Burton	T Cox (returned as teacher)
1944-45	Joyce McDonnell	J Boyce
1945-46	Mary Hart	A D Hutchinson
1946-47	Audrey Kerry	E Roberts (1 term) R Hide
1947-48	Doris Marks	G M Lewis
1948-49	Dorothy Sims	G M Lewis
1949-50	Ruth Adams	R Thornley
1950-51	Joan Lewis	D Harwood
1951-52	Susan Humphreys	E Johnson
1952-53	Mary Jardine	D Hide
1953-54	Shirley Roughley (2 terms) D Ward (2 terms)	
	Nancy Tagg	J Hudson
1954-55	Dilys Hall	B Austin
1955-56	Dilys Hall	A Waddoups
1956-57	Anne Limbert	K Orme

1957–58	Anne Limbert (1.5 terms)	
	Sheila Wright	J Maxwell
1958–59	Phoebe Hall (2 terms)	
	Kathleen Short	D Outram
1959–60	Christine Beswick	D Hilton
1960–61	Kathleen Ward	D Hilton
1961–62	Elizabeth Lyth	P Davis
1962–63	Joan Turner	H Bugg
1963–64	Jeanne Goodson	H Bugg
1964–65	Hilary Teat	C Markham
1965–66	Sylvia Hilton	G Yarrow
1966–67	Kathryn Andrews	D Aichison
1967–68	Vicki Brooks	A Rooth

Space for your own photographs